# Advanced
# Painter™
# Techniques

# Advanced Painter™ Techniques

Don Seegmiller

WILEY PUBLISHING, INC.

Acquisitions Editor: Mariann Barsolo
Development Editor: Stephanie Barton
Technical Editor: Howard Lyon
Production Editor: Elizabeth Ginns Britten
Copy Editor: Karen A. Gill
Production Manager: Tim Tate
Vice President and Executive Group Publisher: Richard Swadley
Vice President and Executive Publisher: Joseph B. Wikert
Vice President and Publisher: Neil Edde
Book Designer and Compositor: Chris Gillespie, Happenstance Type-O-Rama
Proofreader: Nancy Bell
Indexer: Ted Laux
Project Coordinator, Cover: Lynsey Stanford

For general information on our other products and services or to obtain technical support, please contact our Customer Care Department within the
U.S. at (800) 762-2974, outside the U.S. at (317) 572-3993 or fax (317) 572-4002.

Wiley also publishes its books in a variety of electronic formats. Some content that appears in print may not be available in electronic books.

Library of Congress Cataloging-in-Publication Data:

Seegmiller, Don.

 Advanced Painter techniques / Don Seegmiller. — 1st ed.

  p. cm.

 ISBN-13: 978-0-470-28493-3 (paper/website)

 ISBN-10: 0-470-28493-5 (paper/website)

 1. Computer graphics. 2. Fractal Design painter. I. Title.

 T385.S3648 2008

 006.6'86—dc22

                                        2008020135

10 9 8 7 6 5 4 3 2 1

Dear Reader,

Thank you for choosing *Advanced Painter Techniques*. This book is part of a family of premium-quality Sybex books, all of which are written by outstanding authors who combine practical experience with a gift for teaching.

Sybex was founded in 1976. More than 30 years later, we're still committed to producing consistently exceptional books. With each of our titles, we're working hard to set a new standard for the industry. From the paper we print on to the authors we work with, our goal is to bring you the best books available.

I hope you see all that reflected in these pages. I'd be very interested to hear your comments and get your feedback on how we're doing. Feel free to let me know what you think about this or any other Sybex book by sending me an email at nedde@wiley.com, or if you think you've found a technical error in this book, please visit http://sybex.custhelp.com. Customer feedback is critical to our efforts at Sybex.

Best regards,

Neil Edde
Vice President and Publisher
Sybex, an Imprint of Wiley

*This book is dedicated to my family. First and foremost, to my dear wife, Marti; she endured my constant whining about how stressed I was and kept me on track and productive. To my son, Andrew, who had to tolerate the daily ups and downs associated with having a father who works at home. To my daughters, Jenn and Nicole, who have an easier time loving me since they don't have to live with me anymore. And to my parents, who are a constant support and provide encouragement.*

*This is also for all the artists I know and those I have not met who have influenced me either knowingly or not by their work. In addition, I would like to thank all my students over the years. You have taught me more than you will ever know.*

# Acknowledgments

I would like to thank my family. Without their support, I could not have finished this project.

I need to thank David Fugate. Without his help and interest, this project would never have happened.

Thanks to the patient folks at Wiley, in particular Mariann Barsolo and Stephanie Barton. Thanks to Karen Gill; you make my ramblings understandable. And thanks to Liz Britten and the Wiley book-production team for making it all come together.

Howard Lyon, thanks for the fine job you do as my technical editor, catching all my inevitable errors.

# About the Author

**Don Seegmiller** was born in Provo, Utah, in 1955. He grew up in both California and Colorado.

Don graduated Brigham Young University in 1979 with a Bachelor of Fine Arts in graphic design, with a concentration in illustration. After graduation, he decided that he would rather pursue his passion for painting and began a career as an oil painter. While his work has been shown in many major art galleries, the majority of his traditional work is handled by Wadle Galleries Ltd. of Santa Fe. Over the course of the past 30 years, Don's work has been shown worldwide. He has completed close to 1,000 paintings that are included in many private and public collections. His work hangs in the permanent collection of the Springville Museum of Art.

A resident of Orem, Utah, Don lives at the foot of the 11,000-foot-high Mount Timpanogos. He teaches senior-level illustration courses, traditional head painting, figure drawing, and digital painting for the department of visual design at Brigham Young University. He also teaches an upper-division figure drawing class at Utah Valley University.

Don was the art director for six years at Saffire Corp., a well-known game developer in the late 1990s. He has produced art work for many leading game publishers over the years.

A regular speaker at the Game Developers Conference for eight years, Don presented hour-long lectures from 1997 to 2001 and presented full-day tutorials from 2002 to 2005 on character design and digital painting, with bits of creativity thrown in for good measure.

Don was the keynote speaker for the Association of Medical Illustrators at their national convention in the summer of 2003. During the summers of 2004 and 2006, he was invited back to do workshops for the illustrators at the convention. He traveled for a while demonstrating Metacreations Painter 6 at trade shows. Don demonstrates Painter at Corel's booth at major trade shows, in particular Siggraph. His work is featured in the *Painter 6, 7, 8, IX,* and *X Wow Books, Step by Step Electronic Design, Design Graphics,* and both *Spectrum 7* and *8.* He has written tutorials for Corel's release of Painter IX. He was featured both on the Corel web site and in the Painter IX manual.

Don was one of the judges for Ballistic Publishing's Painter book and coauthor for the upcoming *Digital Painting 2* book by the same publisher. He has written the following books: *Digital Character Painting Using Photoshop CS3* (Charles River Media, 2007), *Digital Character Design and Painting: The Photoshop CS Edition* (Charles River Media, 2004), and *Digital Character Design and Painting* (Charles River Media, 2003). He also co-wrote *Mastering Digital 2D and 3D Art* (Thompson Course Technology, 2004).

You can see examples of Don's work at www.seegmillerart.com.

In his free time, Don enjoys fly fishing with his son and riding his motorcycle.

# Contents

# Introduction

*The world is changing in dramatic ways. Not too many years ago, cutting-edge digital art was represented by images created pixel by pixel and limited to 256 colors. Computers that were capable of creating digital art were expensive and pretty unsophisticated compared to today's standards. A 20-megabyte (MB) hard drive was large, and a single megabyte of RAM was $40. I remember well spending $320 to upgrade my computer to 16MB of RAM. And there was no such thing as a stylus to paint with. Every image you created was done with a mouse.*

We've come a long way. Very powerful and capable computers are available for less than $1,000. Hard drives are measured in hundreds of gigabytes (GB), with an average-size 500GB hard drive costing less than $100. RAM is also numbered in gigabytes, with a 4GB stick of RAM costing around $50. And most significantly, there is the tablet and stylus today that make drawing and painting on the computer very similar to writing on a piece of paper.

In the beginning, there were few consumer-oriented programs aimed at the digital artist. The two-dimensional (2D) programs that were available tended to be simple to use but labor intensive when it came to creating an image. The early three-dimensional (3D) programs that were affordable were more like learning a programming language and not intuitive at all to use. I remember the great joy I felt when I successfully rendered my first sphere. Over the years, the number of different applications for creating digital imagery has increased to a point that, no matter what your bent, there is an affordable solution to use to create digital artwork.

Over time, different programs have become the standard in their respective categories. In the 2D raster world, arguably the two major programs are Photoshop and Painter. Photoshop is known as the premier digital image-editing program, and Painter is the top dog when it comes to emulating traditional drawing and painting mediums. Of course, everyone has their favorites, and lively discussion arises when proponents of each get together.

Many books are published each year to teach every feature available in Photoshop. Painter is another story, with only a few instructional books available. I believe that one of the reasons so few books are available about Painter is that the use of the program depends a lot on the individual artist's ability to create a piece of art without relying on special effects, plug-in filters, or clicking on buttons to automate the creation of art. Don't get me wrong; there are many special effects, plug-ins, and buttons to click in Painter, but ultimately the success of the painting depends on the artist.

The reason for this book is to try to merge the creation of art with all the special effects and features that are found in a program like Painter.

Painter has come a long way over the years. From more of a curiosity and hobbyist-based application in its early years to its current incarnation as a full-fledged professional-level program, Painter has never lost its direction as a program that the digital artist can use to simulate traditional art media.

This book, hopefully, will help fill a gap and show how Painter can be used to create digital paintings that would be difficult with another program. It consists of a number of tutorials that merge the creation of art with the power of the program. It offers a balance between drawing and painting and then clicking a button or accessing a plug-in filter. Because so much of the power of Painter is its use by individual artists, the tutorials are written such that artists can follow along using their own sketch or drawing as the base image, but enough detail is written and all the resources used to create each painting provided that artists can also follow along as closely as they would like.

## Who Should Read This Book

Painter is a powerful and sophisticated program with a large set of features and settings available, which can either hamper or help the 2D artist. It is a program that in many ways relies on the artist to really shine. The power available when using Painter is enormous, and there is sometimes the perception that the program will do the work. Like most artistic media, the ultimate quality of the art created is because of the artist, not the tool used. Having said that, the knowledgeable use of Painter's features will not only help increase the quality of already good art, but it will save the artist significant amounts of time, give the artist the ability to paint images that would be hard if not impossible with traditional tools, and hopefully increase the creativity and ability to look at new artistic problems with an increased skill set.

This book is not written as a Painter how-to manual. It is not for readers who are new to Painter. Following the tutorials without a lot of frustration requires a working knowledge of the program. This book is for Painter users who want to add to their knowledge of the application and increase the bag of tricks they have available when painting on the computer.

This book is about some of the techniques that I use to create art with Painter. These techniques are not the only solution to the artistic problems shown but are designed to get the artist thinking about new approaches while showing methods that can be used and adapted to many everyday digital painting problems.

Most books that discuss computer programs used to create digital art rely on explaining what happens when you access this feature, select this menu item, or click this button. This book relies on the artist's own skill meshed with the variety of features found in Painter. It is not an exhaustive exploration of every possible brush, texture, or setting.

This book is for all artists who want to increase their creativity and knowledge of Painter. This includes current Painter users who want to explore different ways to paint a variety of subject matter, Photoshop users who are looking for ways to integrate some of Painter's natural media tools into their workflow, students who may need direction for digital painting classes, and anyone familiar with Painter but unsure how to start creating a digital image from scratch.

Few books are dedicated to digital painting using Painter. Most of the time artists have to search the Internet to find basic Painter information. This can be time consuming and frustrating. It is my hope that this book will provide a comprehensive resource when it comes to techniques used to paint a variety of different subjects.

## What You Will Learn

The chapters in this book are not written in a linear fashion where you must start with Chapter 1 and end with Chapter 9. Each chapter takes a specific subject and shows you ways to paint it using Painter. This is by no means a comprehensive overview of all the ways an artist might approach each type of subject matter but more a demonstration of how I would approach the subject. Thought has been given to demonstrating techniques that can be accomplished relatively quickly. Hopefully, the chapters will trigger new ideas about how the technique used might be adapted to each artist's approach.

## What You Need

You need a working knowledge of Painter to use this book to your greatest advantage. It is assumed that you know the basic operation of the program and where to access different menus and features. If you do not have this knowledge, you might find following along frustrating.

You need a computer that is capable of running Painter; this includes a large hard drive of around 250 gigabytes to save multiple versions of each painting. You should have a stylus and tablet to follow the tutorials; trying to follow along with the mouse would be a lot like painting with a bar of soap. Finally, whether you work on a Mac or PC does not matter, because the programs work virtually the same on each platform.

## What Is Covered in This Book

*Advanced Painter Techniques* is organized to provide you with chapters that show the techniques used to paint specific subject matter. You can start at the beginning and work through to the last chapter, or you can pick individual chapters and work through them in any order. Though different information is presented in each chapter, the knowledgeable Painter user should have no problem moving between chapters.

**Chapter 1: Painting an Image with a 3D Feel**    This chapter covers painting a portrait that has a traditional oil painting look and feel. Painter X has an unsurpassed capability to utilize texture in a variety of ways, some of which are shown here.

**Chapter 2: Painting Clouds, Water, and Stone**    In this chapter, I focus on painting a landscape using Painter X.

**Chapter 3: Painting a Rocky Surface Then Making It Appear Wet**    Here, I use Painter to create several different rocky and wet effects.

**Chapter 4: Painting a Fantasy Forest with the Image Hose**    This chapter is about painting a fantasy forest. I approach creating a forest and foliage in a rather stylistic way, which is not meant to represent reality.

**Chapter 5: Painting the Sleepwalker**    This tutorial features a sleepwalker walking down the middle of a hall in the dead of night. He is carrying a candle to light the way on his nightly travels. In this chapter, I use Painter to create different lighting effects.

**Chapter 6: Painting a Sea Serpent**    This chapter demonstrates how to paint scales on a creature and place him convincingly in his watery element.

**Chapter 7: Painting Red Riding Hood**    This painting of the Red Riding Hood character is pretty straightforward. The tutorial focuses mainly on painting the background using textures, patterns, and custom brushes.

**Chapter 8: From Concept to Complete**    A lot of work that I do is designing characters, creatures, environments, and buildings. In this chapter, we will paint the creature using some of the most typical methods I use when doing this kind of work.

**Chapter 9: Painting Shiny Baubles**    This final chapter is about painting shiny things.

## The Book's Website

All the resource files used in each chapter are available for you to download. This includes any preliminary sketches, paper libraries, pattern libraries, custom brush libraries, and custom lighting presets. To download the files, go to www.sybex.com/go/painter.

## How to Contact the Author

I welcome feedback from you about this book or books you'd like to see from me in the future. You can reach me by writing to donsbook@seegmillerart.com. For more information about my work, please visit my website at www.seegmillerart.com.

Sybex strives to keep you supplied with the latest tools and information you need for your work. Please check this book's website at `www.sybex.com/go/painter`, where we'll post additional content and updates that supplement this book if the need arises.

# Painting an Oil Portrait

*Painter X has an unsurpassed ability to create digital images with a three-dimensional (3D) look and feel. You can use almost any image with Painter X to create a textural effect in a painting. You can create paper libraries, patterns libraries, and an almost-infinite number of brushes, and you can access filter effects that can give an image a 3D look and feel. With Painter X, you are limited only by your creativity and imagination.*

*Painter X allows you to create images that mimic paintings done with traditional media. You can even mix media in nontraditional ways that would be impossible with traditional media; for example, you can create an image that combines watercolor and oil paint.*

**1**

**Chapter Contents**
Creating a 3D Look with 2D Tools
The Result First
Painting the Portrait
Finishing Touches

## Creating a 3D Look with 2D Tools

This chapter is a mix of general painting methods combined with Painter-specific features and techniques. In this chapter, I will show you how to use Painter X to paint a portrait that has the look of a traditional oil painting. You can imitate the 3D effect of oil paint by using many of the tools found in the program. While this chapter will not be an exhaustive look at using these features, it is a good start. We will build on these techniques in subsequent chapters. The actual sequence of steps used for this digital portrait is close to the method I would use to create a traditional oil painting.

I will start by giving an overview of how the entire portrait was painted. To accomplish this, I will show several methods of imitating a 3D surface when working in Painter X. As I demonstrate these methods, you will see the steps used to paint a portrait. Portrait painting is one of the artist's greatest challenges, and having a solid method to follow will help you minimize errors in your own work.

Remember that the subject matter is only a vehicle to show you techniques; you can apply these methods to any subject matter you want. There are, after all, many other types of subject matter that would benefit from the use of texture.

In this and all subsequent chapters, it is assumed that you have a basic understanding of the workings of Painter X. You should know the following things to successfully follow along with the demonstration or take what is presented and experiment on your own:

- Where individual palettes and menu items are located. If certain palettes are not visible at the launch of Painter X, you should know how to access them.
- How to adjust brush settings, including opacity, brush size, and, if needed, bringing up the Brush Creator.
- How to scale the size of the brush and sample colors from within the painting using hot keys. Knowing this speeds up the process and natural flow when you're painting an image.

In Painter X, you can arrange the working space to suit your own way of painting. Because your setup may be different from the default, this chapter will not discuss where to locate specific features and menu items.

In this and subsequent chapters, you will be encouraged to save often and in a sequential fashion. This should become a habit, because it can help you avoid a lot of grief and frustration. In Painter X, simply hold down the Ctrl+Alt+S keys (⌘+Option+S on the Mac) to automatically save the painting with a sequential number added as a suffix to the filename.

## Considering the Result First

The painting we will create is a traditional portrait, where the likeness of the model is the primary consideration. Unlike a traditionally painted oil portrait, where it's necessary to wait for paint to dry to build up a rich surface, the digital painter does not have to worry about wet paint. One of the benefits of working digitally is the speed at which it's possible to create a painting without waiting on materials. The artist can paint, repaint, and overpaint any area at any time as much as necessary to make corrections or change direction entirely.

This tutorial shows you how to use various features found in Painter X to create a painting that imitates the rich and textured surface expected if painting the portrait using oil paint. While it is not an exhaustive demonstration of every technique available in the program, it is extensive in the number of methods shown. We will use different techniques to paint the background, fabric, hair, and flesh.

When we begin painting on the computer, we must first consider the final use of the painting and set up the canvas space accordingly. If the image will be used for print, we need to keep in mind the *dpi* (dots per inch) resolution of the image. While dpi is not important to the computer, it is critical to the printer, and we should set it accordingly to 300. If the plan is to display the image onscreen only, we can leave the dpi at the default setting of somewhere between 72 and 96.

Often, it is best to start with an image that is smaller than the intended final output. Starting small speeds up much of the early work, where details are not important. However, this digital painting technique relies on some early steps involving the use of texture so, in this case, it is better to begin working with the image at its final size. My initial size settings for this tutorial are about 3,000 pixels in each dimension.

> **Note:** All the textures, patterns, and brushes that were used to create the painting are available for download at www.sybex.com/go/painter.

## Setting Up Your Canvas

Let's set up the canvas, apply a texture, and get painting:

1. Create a new image. You can do this in several ways, including using the keyboard shortcut Ctrl+N (⌘+N on the Mac).

2. Change the default resolution if you want, and put **3000** in the Height and Width fields, with Pixels as the unit of measurement.

3. If you have not already done so, use the Pattern Selector menu to either open the Chapter 1 pattern library (Chapter1.ptl) or, using the Pattern Mover, open Chapter1.ptl, click your left mouse button on the gessoed canvas pattern, and drag it over into your default library (Figure 1.1).

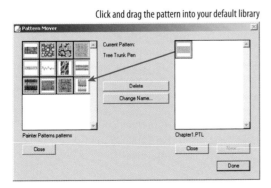

Figure 1.1  The Pattern Mover in Painter X

4. Make sure that the gessoed canvas pattern is active if you have copied it into your default library. If you have just opened chapter1.ptl, you don't need to make changes.

5. Using the Paper Selector, open the Chapter1 paper library. There is only one paper texture in this library, so you may want to append your current default paper library instead of replacing it.

6. In the toolbox, select the Paint Bucket tool (K), make sure that Clone Source is selected in the Tool Property Bar, and fill the image with the gessoed canvas pattern (Figure 1.2). You should have an image that, at 100 percent zoom, has a nice, slightly creamy fill that looks very much like a traditional artist canvas primed with a toned gesso.

7. One last thing, and you will be ready to start painting. In the top menu bar, select Canvas Menu > Surface Lighting. The Surface Lighting controls open (Figure 1.3).

**Figure 1.2**  The new image after being filled with the gessoed canvas pattern

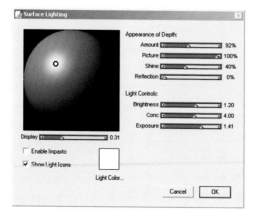

**Figure 1.3**  Controls to make adjustments to the depth effect of the Impasto brushes in Painter X

## Adding Light

Surface Lighting determines the general depth effect of the Impasto Effect in Painter X. The default lighting of this feature is not bad, and for most work it is adequate. Making some slight adjustments to the default settings can add some subtle yet quite beautiful effects to the painting.

Choosing the right direction and color of the light source can add beautiful depth and texture to a stroke. The direction and elevation of the light source can be adjusted by clicking and dragging the small black circle in the middle of the highlight on the sphere.

Take care when changing the position of the light on the virtual globe in the Surface Lighting controls. Placing the light too high on the sphere's surface can wash out the Impasto Effect completely and lighten the entire painting. In contrast, placing the light too low can darken the image and overly exaggerate the Impasto Effect. These settings are global and affect all Impasto brushes on every layer. Figure 1.4 shows the effect of the default setting in the Surface Lighting controls.

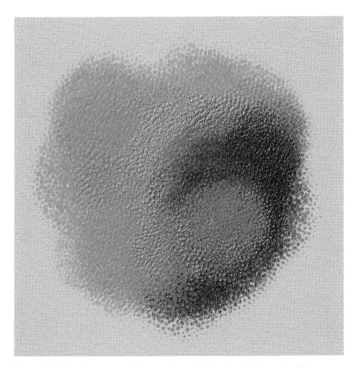

**Figure 1.4** The effect that the default settings of the Surface Lighting controls have on an Impasto brushstroke

For this painting, we will make some changes to the default settings.

1. First, add a second light source. To add a second, third, fourth, or more light source to the image, just click with the cursor anywhere on the sphere. If you make a mistake and add more lights than you want, just click on the small black circle for the light you want to remove and press the Backspace key. You can tell which light is selected because the small circle will appear bold.

Experiment with the position of the light until you are satisfied. A position that is low and to the opposite side of the primary light generally works best.

**2.** Now it's time to change the color of the light. To do this, click on the Light Color square. The system color picker appears, and you can choose any color for the second light source in the painting.

Generally, I find it best to select a darker and more saturated color. Too light a color, and the whole image will look washed out. Because this painting is a traditional portrait and I am fond of complementary color schemes, I select a bluish green color for the secondary light, as you can see in Figure 1.5.

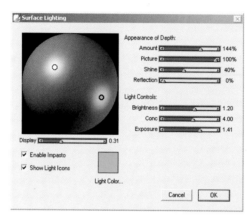

**Figure 1.5** Adding a secondary light source, and setting the color of that light

The effect should be subtle. Looking closely at the enlargement of the earlier brushstroke shows subtle greenish areas in the texture, as in Figure 1.6. Of course, there in no right or wrong when adding more light. Experiment with the controls and become familiar with their use.

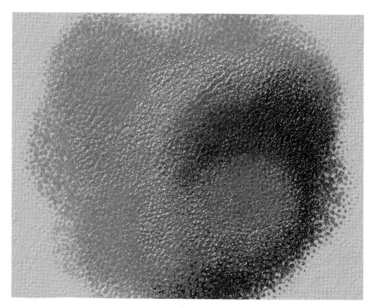

**Figure 1.6** You can see the subtle result of adding a secondary green light source in this close-up of the Impasto brushstroke.

# Painting the Portrait

Now that the preliminary work of setting up the canvas is finished, it is time to begin actually painting the image. Now would also be a good time to save your work.

Most of the time when I start a painting, I do the preliminary sketch in pencil on paper, scan the drawing, and then open the scanned image in Painter X. Occasionally, I draw a sketch for a painting directly in the computer program. I always make sure that the sketch for a painting is on a new layer whether I use a scanned sketch or I draw directly in Painter. Working with layers in this way provides great flexibility in arranging the composition and making corrections to the drawing.

## Drawing the Sketch and Toning the Canvas

In this painting, I quickly drew the sketch in Painter X using one of the brush variants from the Pencils category on a white base. Only the bare essentials of the figure are indicated, because there is the temptation, when using a detailed drawing as the base for a painting, to work in a coloring-book mentality and just fill in the lines. Figure 1.7 shows the sketch that the painting will be based on. Save the sketch.

**Figure 1.7** The sketch for the portrait

First we'll copy the sketch into the image where we'll do the actual painting.

1. Select the whole sketch image, copy it to the Clipboard, and paste it into the prepared canvas.

2. Change the Composite Method of the Sketch layer to Multiply, and move the sketch around until its placement in the new image is satisfactory.

3. When you are happy with the composition, you can equalize the Sketch layer to get rid of the gray areas of the sketch if they are distracting. Typically, you would use the Equalize effect to place the black-and-white points and then evenly distribute the gray values between the two. Here, Equalize is used to eliminate some of the gray values by moving the white point indicator down into the gray areas. You can find the Equalize adjustments in the Effects menu, under Tonal Control. Figure 1.8 shows where to find Equalize.

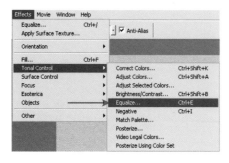

**Figure 1.8** The location of the Equalize command

4. Move the Brightness slider and White Point indicator slightly to the left. The image updates as you move the sliders so that you can preview the effect (Figure 1.9).

The image will look something like Figure 1.10.

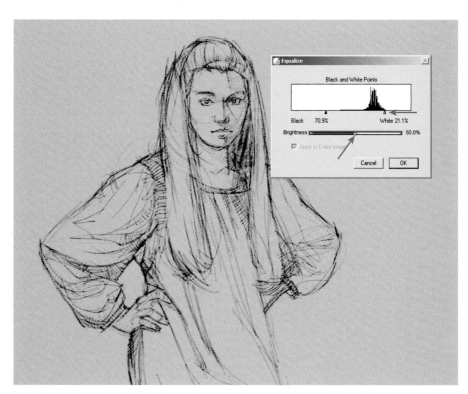

**Figure 1.9** Previewing the image as you adjust with Equalize

**Figure 1.10** The Sketch layer is equalized, put in place, and ready for the next step.

5. Save the image using the Iterative Save command (Ctrl+Alt+S on the PC or ⌘+Option+S on the Mac). When saving from this point forward, use this command, which creates a new file with a numeric suffix. The advantage is that multiple files are created should you need to revert to an earlier version.

**Note:** All the brushes used in this painting are available for download as a zip file called Book Brushes.zip. at www.sybex.com/go/painter. You should have all of them installed and ready to use for the remainder of this tutorial. If you need help installing the brushes, please refer to the Painter help file.

When you paint with traditional media (except watercolor), it is often wise to paint on a mid-value ground. All colors look dark when you paint against a white ground, and that can make it hard for you to correctly judge the relationship between the light and dark values in your paintings. Using a toned ground may be even more important when you are working with digital media, because the white of the screen is so intensely bright.

Traditional media use pigment. Pigmented paint is much darker than paint made of light—which is basically what is happening on a computer. The whites are bright on a computer screen, and the value differences can be greater.

If you paint on a white canvas, eventually you will cover the surface entirely with paint, and you can then correctly judge the difference between the values of the colors. Often, though, you must adjust the colors and values that you paint in the early stages. You can avoid unnecessary repainting by toning the painting surface before you place the first stroke.

### Toning the Canvas

You can use various methods to change the value and color of a blank canvas before painting on the computer. Filling the area with a color using the Paint Bucket tool is often enough. For this particular project, though, we want the look and feel of a traditional oil painting, and a simple fill will not suffice. Also, the canvas already has some color and a pattern that we don't want to cover. The solution is to use one of Painter X's Watercolor brushes to paint a darker tone across the canvas. The effect will be the same as a coating of thinned oil paint brushed over a canvas.

**1.** Select the Canvas Toner brush variant.

**2.** Choose a dark brownish color, and paint a series of sweeping strokes across the canvas.

Because we are using a Watercolor brush, it will create its own new layer. Figure 1.11 shows the painting with a darker color painted over the figure and into the background, leaving a wet look.

**Figure 1.11** The painting with a darker wash painted over the sketch using the Canvas Toner brush

There is no need to worry about covering the underlying sketch since the Watercolor layer defaults to a Gel Composite Method, similar to Multiply, and lighter colors become progressively more transparent. The strokes will run and diffuse into the canvas paper texture. In Figure 1.12, the close-up of the painting shows how the color puddles and runs into the canvas texture.

**Figure 1.12**  Watercolor diffuses into the paper texture.

Note that even though you paint with the Watercolor brush on its own layer above the Canvas layer, the brush and the paper texture interact as if you were painting on the canvas.

The Watercolor brushes in Painter are processor intensive. If you have a slower computer, you may see some lag to the brushstroke as you paint. This is not a technical problem, but it can be rather annoying. If you experience some lag, try increasing the Boost setting using the slider in the Brush Creator. You can access the Brush Creator using the Ctrl+B (⌘+B on the Mac) keys. You will find the Boost control under the General tab of the Stroke Designer. Sometimes increasing the percent of Boost dramatically improves performance when you paint with the Watercolor brushes (Figure 1.13).

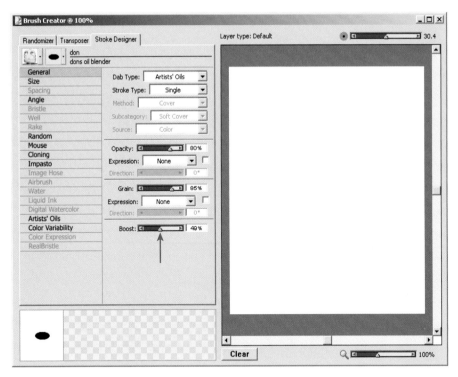

**Figure 1.13** The Boost control slider

### Blocking in the Base Colors

In traditional opaque painting, it is good practice to paint from darker to lighter colors in large and fairly rough shapes. That's a process I continue to use when I paint with the computer.

At this stage in the painting, the image often looks way too rough and sloppy, but it is not meant to be finished work. The early stage of adding color to a painting is called *block-in*. Blocking in color involves the simple process of roughly putting colors in the correct values and in the correct spot in the painting. There is no finesse or attempt to blend these colors. Blocking in the large shapes only establishes the basic building blocks to be refined later.

Before blocking in the colors, we need to rearrange some of the layers.

1. Click in the Layers palette on the Watercolor layer, and drag it down until it is the first layer above the canvas.

2. Click the Add Layer button at the bottom of the Layers palette, use the Layers menu, or use the keys Ctrl+Shift+N (⌘+Shift+N on the Mac) to create a new layer right above the Watercolor layer. Make sure the Preserve Transparency box is not checked, and check the Pick Up Underlying Color box.

3. Change to the Brush tool if it is not already active (B key), and pick the Captured Bristle brush variant in the Acrylics brush category. This default brush is a great one to use to block colors in quickly in the initial stages of a painting. It has a brushy feel to the strokes, is opaque, and has a bristly appearance.

4. Choose a dark color and block in the dark areas of the painting on the new layer. Go ahead and use the same dark color to paint not only the fabric, but also some of the darker areas in the hair. Figure 1.14 shows this initial block-in of the dark color, as well as the arrangement of the various layers.

5. Using the same brush, continue to paint in the colors of the fabric, gradually moving to lighter colors. In the case of a deep red fabric, as in this painting, take care not to go too light with the red. Red is one of the only colors that will eventually become a different color as it is lightened. You do not want a pink costume.

**Figure 1.14** Painting in with a darker color on a new layer using the Captured Bristle Acrylic brush

Notice that some of the red also is painted over the edges of the sketch extending into the background. This apparent mess is intentional. A bit of foreground color painted into the background helps unify the color scheme. The reverse is also true. A bit of the background color brought into some of the foreground figure helps harmonize the color scheme even more. Figure 1.15 shows that most of the dress is now blocked in with red.

**Figure 1.15**  Most of the red color is blocked into the dress.

6. Continuing with the same brush, paint the face with a flesh color and the hair with a blonde color.

In this painting, I've tried to keep the model's hair really light to give it a nice contrast against her darker dress. Paint strokes of color across the forms in the face to give some volume to the features. A lot of color from the background is finding its way into the colors of the hair. This is intentional to help unify the color harmonies, as mentioned previously (Figure 1.16).

All of this color work is beneath the Sketch layer, as you can see in Figure 1.16. Because of the overlying sketch and the rough handling of the color, the painting is in a pretty ugly stage right now. Don't get discouraged if you think your painting is ugly. Virtually all paintings go through an ugly phase early on and will improve if the artist does not give up on it.

7. Without changing the brush but only varying the size and extensive use of the Dropper tool, block in the background colors.

The need to go back to the Colors palette for new colors will gradually diminish. Most colors needed to complete the painting will already be in the painting when you are finished with the block-in.

**Figure 1.16** Here you can see the block-in of color for the face and hair.

## Enhancing the Oil Painting Texture

To give the painting the appearance of an oil painting, we need to add more texture to the 3D illusion.

1. Create a new layer above the Sketch layer. Some of the original sketch will be covered while you paint on this layer.

2. Pick the Variable Chalk variant from the Chalk category. This is a brush that ships with Painter X; you don't need to change any of its default settings other than size as you paint. The brush is good for painting textured surfaces. Because the paper texture that is active is gessoed canvas, the brushstrokes painted with this brush look as if they are painted on a canvas surface.

3. Use the Dropper tool to sample color from different areas in the canvas and paint large and bold strokes of color with the Variable Chalk brush. Work the strokes up close to the figure, and don't worry if there is the occasional overlap into the figure, as you can see on the right elbow of the model in the painting (Figure 1.17).

   The nature of this particular brush is very different from the Acrylic brush that we used earlier. As we continue to build up color with the Variable Chalk brush, a softness and subtle blending begins to show, while interacting nicely with the paper texture.

4. Work all over the background of the painting to create a rich and textured surface.

   Now we need to make a major change in the painting. To mimic the look and feel of an oil painting, we need to do the remainder of the work on one layer.

5. Before moving on, make sure you do an iterative save so you can recover to this spot if anything goes wrong in the next step.

**Figure 1.17** The background is painted using the Variable Chalk brush.

We need to paint on one layer to temper the nature of the Impasto brushes that we will use. These brushes create their impasto effect on any layer where they are applied. Building on multiple layers tends to make the impasto effect on each succeeding layer shinier. While shine might be a good thing in some cases, it is not desirable for this painting. Figure 1.18 shows how the shine in the impasto effect builds from the Canvas layer on the left to the purple color on the right, which is painted on a fourth layer.

**Figure 1.18** The progressive shine of the Impasto effect as it is painted on four layers

**6.** Drop all the layers onto the canvas, and save the image once again.

The painting in general is rough, and the dark sketch lines are dominant. To slightly soften the roughness of the painting and start to subordinate the sketch lines, we need to do a bit of blending. The blending should be subtle so it doesn't obliterate the colors and values that are already established in the painting.

7. Select the Dons Grainy Water brush, and set the Opacity slider to 15 percent. Using a light touch, blend and soften the edges in the painting. In some areas of the painting, blend along the edge to keep it crisp; in other areas, blend across the edge to soften the transition between colors and values.

Follow these general guidelines on how to handle blending and edges: keep the edges sharper and with less blending in the areas of the painting where you want the center of interest to be. Also make sharper the edges of small forms and forms that are strongly lit. The edges in areas of less interest can be softer. The edges in shadows and on large forms can also be blended more.

The blending will have an immediate result in making the painting look even worse than earlier versions. Don't worry; this is a normal precursor to finishing the painting. Figure 1.19 shows the painting after blending. The dark sketch lines are now significantly reduced in strength and opacity. Some of the edges where the figure meets the background are very soft, with color from the figure spilling into the background and vice versa. The edges of the hair are blended into the fabric and background, giving a soft base to later finish the hair on.

**Figure 1.19** Using Dons Grainy Water brush to blend and soften the painting. Notice that the dark sketch lines are not nearly as strong now.

This is the end of the block-in stage of the painting. The basic colors and values are now established and, in many ways, you've completed the most important stage of a painting. For all practical purposes, the look of the painting is now established. From this point on, the work is meant to refine what is painted.

### Refining the Portrait

The block-in is a relatively easy phase of the painting process that quickly sets the tone for the painting. Most of the work is just beginning. The finish takes those early building blocks and refines them.

Most of the painting is going to be done with Impasto brushes. You can find all the brushes used in the painting in the Chapter 1 brush library.

There are a few things you should be aware of as you paint using Impasto brushes:

- You can turn the Impasto effect on and off to view the painting without the 3D effect. Sometimes this is valuable when you're working on small details in the painting. To temporarily turn off the Impasto Effect, just click on the Toggle Impasto Effect button. It is the small blue star in the upper-right corner of the document window. Then click the star again to turn the Impasto Effect back on. The appearance of the shape will either look flat if the Impasto Effect is off or look 3D if the Impasto Effect is on (Figure 1.20).

**Figure 1.20**  The Toggle Impasto Effect icon to turn the Impasto Effect on and off

- When you move the painting around in the document window, you may feel a bit of lag as the image redraws. When zooming in and out, you may also experience some redraw problems with areas of the image that did not zoom in or out correctly (Figure 1.21). If you find this a nuisance, click the Toggle Impasto Effect button temporarily off. The redraw issues are caused by the computer processor trying to keep up drawing the effect as you move the image around in real time; sometimes it just can't keep up.

- You might want to turn off the impasto effect while you paint. Areas of fine detail are often easier to paint if Impasto is temporarily turned off.

- At times, too much impasto is visible, and it distracts from the painting. Should this be the case, you can use the brush called Depth Equalizer to remove some of the impasto depth. This is a default Painter X brush and found in the Impasto category. Use it carefully, or you can remove too much too quickly. Included in the Chapter1 brushes is my own variant of the brush that I think is a bit easier to use.

**Figure 1.21** A strange redraw problem when zooming the image with Impasto turned on

There is no correct way to approach the painting process from this point on; you may have a method that works better for your particular style. My usual process is to work from the dark to the light. I also move around the image working on different areas as I finish the painting. If you're following along, let's continue.

1. Select the Dons Oil 3 brush. This is a fine-bristled brush that was made to work on smaller areas with only a bit of the Impasto effect visible. It is the perfect brush to paint the face of the portrait. Leave the brush at the default settings to begin.

2. Paint and refine the features in the face. Place the brushstrokes across the forms in the face to give a sense of roundness. The direction of the brushstrokes is clearly

visible in Figure 1.22. You need to pick some colors from the Colors palette, and others you can sample using the Dropper tool from different areas in the painting. Some dark reds from the dress are placed in the deep shadow areas of the face and hair. Bright oranges are placed under the chin. Background greens and golds are used in the shadow areas of the face and hair. The most obvious green is on the shadow side of the chin and cheek.

3. Using a lighter pressure with this brush gives you a smaller stroke, enabling you to paint smaller areas and details. Loosely paint the features in the face without changing the brush size.

4. Paint the detail in her hair. The strokes used to paint her hair follow the flow of her hair.

5. Switch to Dons Opaque Oil 2 brush. This brush is similar to the brush you just used, with a few modifications. The most important difference is that the number of bristles is larger, giving a smoother and thicker stroke. Brushes that have many bristles are quite processor intensive, so you should take care when using them at large sizes. Too large of a brush, and a significant lag will accompany the stroke.

6. Paint the hair, and begin to paint the background using the brush. All colors are sampled from the image at this point. This brush is covering the canvas texture created in the block-in stage. That's okay since traditional oil paint often does cover the texture of the canvas it is painted on. The goal is to begin to produce strokes that have the thick, wet feel of real oil paint. There is also some subtle impasto starting to show in the hair (Figure 1.22).

**Figure 1.22** Early details are painted into the face using Don's Oil brush. You can also see the thick and wet quality of the strokes painted in the hair.

**7.** Switch brushes again and pick Dons Oils. This is a large brush made for painting large and rough strokes into the background of an image. The Impasto setting of this brush makes the strokes look 3D and gives a nice thick-paint feel to the areas where it is used.

Now the fun begins. Using colors selected from the background, paint some bold strokes back into the background. Use short and choppy strokes to start. This brush will cover most of the canvas texture from earlier steps, but do not paint into the corners of the image where the light areas of the canvas are still visible. Some of the canvas texture needs to be visible in the corners for later in the process. Notice that the harder the pressure is on the stylus, the more pronounced the impasto. Enjoy experimenting with the brush. There is no right or wrong way to paint in the background. The result is to create the look and feel of paint built up on the canvas (Figure 1.23).

**Figure 1.23** Dons Oils brush can be used to create thickly textured areas in a painting.

**8.** Pick the brush Dons Oils 2. This brush is similar to Dons Oils except that it is better for longer and more decorative strokes.

Paint into the background areas that border the fabric of the dress. Using longer strokes and varying the direction, begin to build up areas that look very much like thick paint. Varying amounts of pressure affect the depth and size of the stroke.

Move on to the dress and, using the Dropper to pick the color, start with the darker areas of the fabric and paint some nice thick strokes. I generally paint across the form of the dress just as in the face to add dimension to the folds (Figure 1.24).

A few of the original sketch strokes are still visible in the hands and hair, but most have been covered by this time. The rest will be covered shortly.

**Figure 1.24** Using Dons Oil 2 to paint in the background and move into the dress of the figure

**9.** Using the same brush, add long strokes of color to the hair. Take care to make sure that the strokes of the brush conform to the direction that the hair flows. The impasto of the stroke helps the illusion of painted hair (Figure 1.25).

Much of the work in the next few images is just a matter of moving around the image, switching brushes, and continuing to refine the painting. If there is any step that is unusual, I will describe the technique. Otherwise, the only changes to the brushes will be increasing their size up or down. Follow along so you can see how the work is done, but for the time being, there are no shortcuts or special techniques other than just painting.

**Figure 1.25** Large impasto strokes are painted in the hair using Dons Oils 2.

10. Moving back to paint on the face, switch brushes to Dons Opaque Oil 2. This brush has more small bristles and is just the thing for more delicate work. Continue to build the colors of the face carefully, trying to get a bit more finish. The strokes of the brush are still being built up across the forms as they start to blend together visually. There is no blending going on other than that which happens as the brushstrokes overlap.

It is never good to complete one area of a painting and then move on to the next. It is better to move constantly around trying to bring the whole image to completion at the same time. If you paint one area at a time, there is a good chance that the painting as a whole will not work well visually. The color might be spotty, or the values may be off. There are any number of small problems that arise when focusing on small areas. In the end, you will find yourself moving around and trying to make fixes and adjustments. Too narrow a focus is particularly hard in digital painting, where you are able to zoom into one particular area for work without seeing the rest of the painting.

11. Use the same brush that you used to paint the face—Dons Opaque 2—to paint the hands. Because the hands are not the center of interest, more impasto is built up as they are painted. Impasto can become distracting, so it's best to keep it to a minimum in the face and use it with more abandon everywhere else.

Also, paint some of the background around the hands. Paint the tips of the fingernails using a light background color. Then add some bright and slightly magenta color to the fabric by the hands. This is the lightest red color that will be used in the dress; going much lighter could push the color toward pink (Figure 1.26).

**Figure 1.26** Painting on the hands, background, and fabric

**12.** Overall, the painting is coming along nicely. Continue to do more work on the face, dress, and background. Add a hairclip on the top of her head. Figure 1.27 shows the entire painting at this point.

**Figure 1.27** The complete painting after work on the face, dress, and background

The painting is finished enough that we can add some of the smaller details. Adding detail is always a bit tricky. Too much, and the painting will look overworked. Too few, and a painting can look unfinished.

**13.** Move back to the hair and pick the Dons Oil 3 brush. Because this brush will paint with smaller bristles when using less pressure on the stylus, not much resizing is necessary. Paint in some smaller strands of hair in both the shadow and light side of the hair. Use the Dropper to select the right colors. Be careful not to overdo the number of small strands of hair that are painted. Too many, and the effect will be artificial. Figure 1.28 shows the smaller strands of hair painted into the larger hair masses.

**Figure 1.28** Smaller strands of hair painted into the larger hair masses using the Dons Oil 3 Brush

14. Finish the hand. There is not nearly as much detail put into the hand as the face. Paint colors from the dress into the fingers and into the shadow areas. The addition of the red color warms the hand and harmonizes with the dress. Hands are quite red naturally, so the addition of the red lends reality to the painting (Figure 1.29).

15. The figure is nearly finished. Add a few small details, such as small strands of hair falling over the forehead (Figure 1.30).

**Figure 1.29** Finishing the painting of the hands

**Figure 1.30** The figure is generally finished, with a few small details added, like the hair over the forehead.

## Finishing Touches

At some point, an image can stand on its own and be called finished. This painting has reached a point where I could probably call it finished. There are just a few more things I want to do to help polish the piece. These things include

- Working in the background corners just a bit more to make the area look like canvas.

- Giving the overall painting just a few touches here and there to refine the look of an oil painting. Mostly this will be adding back in some of the canvas texture.

- Setting the painting aside for a few days and then looking at it with a fresh eye. There are small areas needing additional work in every painting that often are overlooked simply because of an artist's fatigue when looking at their own work. Not looking at an image for several days can give you a fresh outlook. While not exactly a part of the painting finish, this is critical to producing the best painting possible.

First we need to fine-tune the two lower corners of the painting to make sure that the canvas looks as if it has been painted over with oil paint. Figure 1.31 shows the bottom-right corner of the painting.

This area does not look too bad. The canvas texture shows well in the corner, and the painted textures show up well as you get closer to the figure. If possible, though, I would like to have the paint look more like it was dry brushed over the canvas texture. Here is how to go about creating the dry brush look:

1. Select the Dons Oil Scumble brush. This brush will dramatically interact with the paper texture. Using the Dropper tool, select the light canvas color in the bottom-right corner of the painting, and paint some rough strokes into the textured areas.

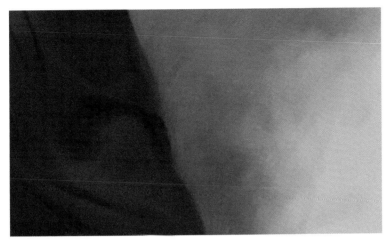

**Figure 1.31** The bottom-right corner of the painting as it currently appears

2. Invert the paper texture in the Papers palette. To do this, just click on the Invert Paper button. Figure 1.32 shows the location of this button in the Papers palette.

3. Select a color from within the painted and textured area, and paint back into the canvas corner. The result should look something like Figure 1.33.

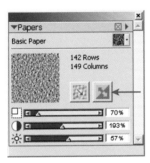

**Figure 1.32** The location of the Invert Paper button on the Papers palette

**Figure 1.33** Using the Dons Oil Scumble brush, light color is painted into the darker textured area, and textured color is painted into the canvas corner.

4. Clone the image by using the Clone command located in the File menu. The cloned image appears and becomes the active image, with the original behind it. It is interesting to note that when an image is cloned, the Impasto effect is flattened down into the painting. The small star button no longer has an effect when you click on it.

5. Close the original image. Save the clone image with a new sequential name, and clone the new image once again. You should now have the original clone and a clone of the clone.

6. With the clone image active, select Surface Control > Apply Surface Texture from the Effects menu (Figure 1.34).

7. The Apply Surface Texture box has many options. Move the Amount slider down to about 32% and the Shine slider to 0%, and then click OK (Figure 1.35). The canvas texture is applied to the entire surface of the cloned image (Figure 1.34).

8. Save and rename the cloned image. Do not close it. In the File menu, go to Clone Source, and make sure the textured image is selected with a check by its name. Minimize the painting so it is out of the way.

**Figure 1.34** The Apply Surface Texture menu item

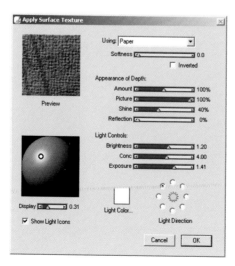

**Figure 1.35** The available commands in the Apply Surface Texture options box

**Figure 1.36** The cloned image with the canvas texture applied

9. Choose the Soft Cloner brush from the Cloning Brushes category, and clone the rough, textured image back into the corner of the painting (Figure 1.37). There is now a much more convincing transition from the rough canvas texture of the canvas into the painted textures.

10. Carefully, and with a light touch, clone a bit of the canvas textured painting back into the original. This mimics convincingly the effect of canvas showing through the paint here and there in a traditional oil painting.

11. In a traditional painting, the dark passages are usually thinner paint than the lighter areas, so it is particularly appropriate to clone back in some of the canvas textures in the darker areas (Figure 1.38).

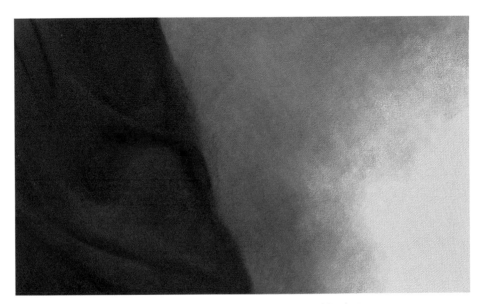

**Figure 1.37** The textured clone source is painted back into the lower-right corner of the painting.

**Figure 1.38** The result of cloning some canvas textured areas back into the original painting

The painting is now looking quite convincing and really could be considered finished. However, a bit more texture in the background would contrast nicely with the smoother areas of the face. We can add this texture easily using one additional brush.

**12.** Select the Oil Splatter 2 brush from the brush picker. This brush is a captured dab brush that has been customized so it will resemble splattered paint.

**13.** Create a new layer and, selecting colors from within the background, paint some splatter textures. Paint as many or as few as you like. Do not worry about the edges of the figure. Because the strokes are being painted on a new layer, any splatter that covers the edges of the figure can be erased (Figure 1.39).

**14.** Once you have erased the edges, drop the textured layer onto the canvas.

A few minor changes are made to the edges of the figure. Then I add my signature on a new layer, and the painting is done. Figure 1.40 shows the complete and finished painting.

**Figure 1.39** Painting with the Oil Splatter brush produces some interesting textures. The rough parts that overlap the figure will be erased.

**Figure 1.40** The finished painting

## Final Thoughts

While the subject matter of this tutorial was a portrait, the real reason for doing this tutorial was to show some of the many ways that texture can be added and used in a digital painting. A few approaches we used in this painting included

- Filling an image with a texture made from a photograph

- Painting with Impasto brushes

- Applying a surface texture to an image

There are as many ways to apply a texture as there are reasons for wanting to use texture in a painting. In this case, we wanted to make something created on the computer look as if it were created with traditional media.

The techniques demonstrated here will not replace a good painting, and you should not rely on them to rescue a work of art. When used in conjunction with good art skills, textures can give your painting that little extra something.

In subsequent chapters, we will use more texture techniques, but I hope that this first chapter will fire your imagination to try new and original approaches as you paint.

# Painting Clouds, Water, and Stone

2

*Painting a landscape seems like a simple task; after all, the major elements do not move. Some elements in the landscape, however, can prove difficult to paint in a believable manner. In this chapter, I will demonstrate one method of painting such elements as clouds, water, and rocks.*

*In this tutorial, you will also see me change my mind, back up, and head in a different direction. Often art tutorials make the process seem so clean and straightforward that readers wonder why they can't make it work the same way. I always like to include a chapter or two where you see the mistakes and course adjustments.*

**Chapter Contents**

## Learning the Fundamentals of Painting a Landscape

This chapter is a mix of general painting methods and Painter-specific tricks and techniques. While no program can substitute for good artistic training, Painter X has many features that can simplify painting a difficult subject matter.

In this demonstration, Painter's brushes, plug-in layers, fractal pattern generator, and other features ease the creative process. You will use such features to make quick work of tedious painting tasks. You will also use custom brushes for most of the work; these are available for download.

There is no right or wrong way to paint a landscape, as artists will adopt their own particular method. There are, however, methods and techniques that can save you time and effort and may improve your painting method.

My approach in this demonstration varies from the way I usually paint. I have tried to break the individual subjects into their own sections and paint from start to finish on each. But I had only marginal success doing this, as some areas depended on the completion of others. In particular, to finish the water portion of the painting, I had to finish the rocks, so a bit of bouncing around was inevitable. When I paint in my usual fashion, I tend to work all around the painting rather than finishing any one section ahead of the others.

Remember that the subject matter is only a vehicle to show the technique used. You can apply the general methods to any subject matter you want.

## Painting the Clouds

Clouds always seem to be a problem for the landscape artist. First of all, they move, constantly change shape, and generally don't give you enough time to accurately draw them. Of course, a cloud will stay still in a photograph. Often, though, if you simply copy a photograph, the cloud will look static and not have the fleeting and insubstantial characteristics that are so important when painting clouds.

While there are many different types of clouds, this exercise will concentrate on the large and fluffy cumulonimbus variety. These are the clouds that reach high into the atmosphere and are often associated with storm fronts. They are also my favorite type of cloud to paint.

It is usually better to paint the impression of clouds rather than try to copy them, so that is the approach in this painting where no reference for the clouds is used.

 **Note:** All the paper textures, patterns, and brushes that were used to create this painting are available to download at www.sybex.com/go/painter.

Before we paint, we need to create a new canvas to paint on and prepare it for the rest of the session.

**1.**     Create a new image using the keyboard shortcut Ctrl+N (⌘+N on the Mac).

2. Change the default resolution to **300** dpi (dots per inch) if you plan to print your image, and enter **900** in the Height box and **1200** in the Width box. Make sure that your unit of measurement is pixels and not inches.

3. Because this will be a landscape painting, fill the canvas with a mid-value blue color. A mid-value color would generally be too dark for a sky, but because this will be a sunset scene, the sky can be significantly darker.

4. Large expanses of flat color are boring visually and boring to paint on, so go ahead and add a Lighting effect to make the sky a bit more interesting.

   The Lighting effect is in the Effects > Surface Control menu. The Apply Lighting options box opens where you can select and preview a number of lighting schemes before applying them to the canvas. In this case, we'll probably paint over the entire canvas, so it's not critical which lighting preset you choose. Choose the Splashy Color preset and click OK. Figure 2.1 shows the Apply Lighting controls.

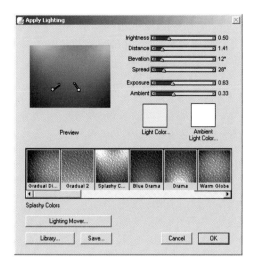

**Figure 2.1** The Apply Lighting options and controls

Now is a good time to save your work. Make sure that you get in the habit of saving your painting frequently. Frequently backing up the painting can save you a lot of grief in later stages when you may want to go back to an earlier version and make corrections or change the direction of the painting. Saving often also protects you against the occasional act of God, like unexpected thunderstorms that can cause power outages.

Save the image.

Now that the canvas is more interesting to look at with nice warm and cool gradations across the image, let's begin painting.

Usually when I start a painting, I draw a preliminary sketch, but in this case I really have no concrete idea of what the image is going to look like, so there is no initial sketch. All I know is that there will be a sky at sunset with some water and rocks in the foreground. For this painting, we will work on individual layers and progress from the farthest elements in the image painted on the lower layers to the nearest pictorial elements on the top layers.

1.    Create a new layer for painting the clouds. Name the layer Clouds.

   Get in the habit of naming the layers you create. In an image that will have as few layers as this one, naming is less important, but some images may have many layers. It can become hard to find a specific layer if they are all named Layer1, 2, 3, and so on.

2.    When you create a new layer, always check the Pick Up Underlying Color box so your brushstrokes will interact with the colors in underlying layers. Of course, the amount of interaction with the underlying color depends on which particular brush you use. Some brushes interact more than others, but it is a good habit to make sure this box is checked regardless. If you don't check the box initially, it is not a critical mistake since you can check it at any time, but you may get some brushstrokes that do not behave as you expect.

3.    Using Dons Brush set to a low Opacity setting of 20%, paint in some big masses of color for the base of the sunlit clouds. Vary the color, intensity, and value of these initial strokes. Concentrate lighter and more intense colors at the top of the cloud shapes and less intense darker colors at the bottom.

**Note:** All the brushes are available for download in a zip file called Book Brushes.zip. You should have all of them installed and ready to use for the remainder of the tutorial. If you need help installing the brushes, please refer to the Painter help file.

Because we have no cloud reference, the shapes and placement of the strokes are not critical. You do want to consider the eventual direction of the light in the painting and paint the strokes accordingly. In this case, the light will enter from the right and slightly in front of the scene, and the cloud shapes are painted accordingly. Figure 2.2 shows the loose conglomeration of brushstrokes that will eventually become clouds.

4.    Using the same brush but at a smaller size, begin to refine the cloud shapes a bit more. There appears to be more detail, yet there really is not. I am simply building on the earlier image to solidify the shapes of my clouds a bit while still maintaining the option of changing anything or everything.

   The word *refining* can sound ambiguous. When I say *refine*, I am starting to have a clearer mental vision of what I want these clouds to look like, and I start to paint that vision with a bit more detail. Yet because I want to keep the painting process fluid and subject to revision and change, I try to keep away from too much detail early in this process. Almost invariably when adding specifics and fine details to a painting early on, these details will be wrong, but because you spent so much time painting them, changing them can be hard mentally as well as technically.

   Figure 2.3 shows the refining process. Notice that darker colors are added into what will be the shadow side of the clouds and in their bases to give some weight to the forms.

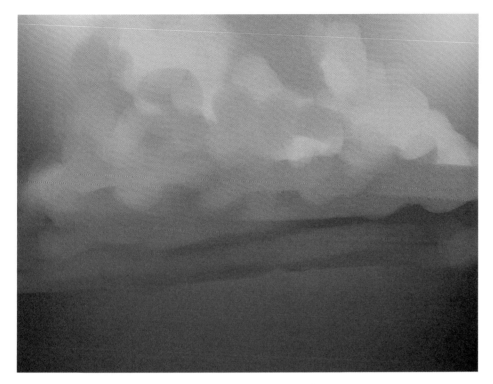

**Figure 2.2** Large, random brushstrokes that will eventually represent clouds in the painting

**Figure 2.3** Smaller and not quite as random brushstrokes are used to add more darks and lights into the cloud shapes, giving them a bit more dimension and weight.

Clouds are not usually thought of as having weight because they float in the sky. But painting them without thought to their form and weight usually results in clouds that really don't look like clouds.

## Defining the Horizon

Now that we have painted the basic color and shape of the clouds, we need to determine where the horizon line will lie. While a horizon line is not critical to the clouds in this painting, it will be important later when we paint the water and rocks.

1.   To define the future horizon line, use the rectangular selection tool and drag a selection on the Cloud layer encompassing everything from the horizon to the bottom of the painting.

2.   Use the Backspace key to clear this part of the layer of any painted strokes. Figure 2.4 shows the layer with the bottom section deleted. The horizon line is now defined by the bottom of the painted strokes.

**Figure 2.4** A horizon line is determined by selecting the bottom portion of the cloud layer and pressing the Backspace key to delete any painted strokes.

## Creating Fluffy Clouds

Now it is time to do some serious cloud painting. In the brushes associated with this book are three brushes called Cloud, Cloud2, and Cloud3. You can use each of these custom brushes to paint nice fluffy clouds with some ease.

1.   If the Brush tool is not currently active, select it by clicking on the Brush icon in the toolbox or pressing the B key. Pick the Cloud Variant in the Book Brushes brush category; the Brush Selector is in the upper-right corner of the Painter

workspace. The Cloud Variant brush is a great cloud-painting brush. You'll do most of the painting in the clouds with it.

> **Note:** When you paint, remember to use the shortcut keys to size and pick colors. Ctrl+Alt (Option+⌘ on the Mac) resizes the brush interactively. Hold the keys down and drag in the painting window. A circle interactively changes size, indicating the size of your brush. When the size is what you want, release the keys. The Alt key (Option on the Mac) activates the Dropper tool, which you can use to select colors quickly and easily.

2. Choose a color that is lighter than the lightest cloud color currently in the painting. Then resize the brush so it is rather small. In this particular painting, a brush size from 10–20 will be most useful.

3. Using short and circular brushstrokes, paint into the edges of one of the main cloud shapes. The stroke should consist of many small circular motions that form a larger somewhat-spiral shape. The brushstroke will start out in the currently selected color and quickly fade into the surrounding colors. Figure 2.5 shows the type of motion to use when you paint the brushstroke (but using a large brush for clarity). If you look closely, you can see the many small strokes overlapping and painted into a somewhat spiral shape.

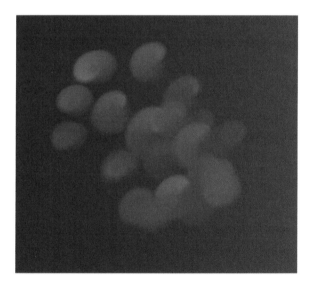

**Figure 2.5** Small circular brushstrokes are painted over themselves in a roughly spiral shape.

Learning to use the Cloud Variant brush successfully takes some practice but is worth the effort. With this brush, it is possible to paint a cloudy shape with light or dark areas in the deep canyon, like areas you see in large clouds. Figure 2.6 shows an extreme close-up of the edge of the cloud shape as lighter colors are painted over the existing colors. Notice the deep but light valley-like area. This is painted using the small circular strokes mentioned before and overlapping them with later strokes.

This technique works best if painted from the top outside edges to the lower middle of the cloud shape.

**Figure 2.6** A close-up of the edge of the cloud shape as lighter colors are painted over the existing colors using a circular motion with the cloud brush

Because we are not using a reference to paint the clouds, our goal is to paint the impression of the clouds and not the actual cloud itself.

4. Paint the rest of the clouds starting with larger brushstrokes and a larger size brush. Use lighter colors to begin the brushstroke.

5. As the light color fades, without lifting the stylus, continue to make the circular brushstrokes back over the lighter colors. The forms of the clouds will begin to appear in your brushstrokes without much effort. Figure 2.7 shows how the Cloud Variant brush has been used in larger sizes to paint the larger shapes of the clouds over the underlying colors.

**Figure 2.7** Using large circular strokes along with larger brush sizes, the entire cloud is painted over the underlying base colors.

In some cases, these larger strokes will be convincing enough in the imitation of a bank of clouds that you can stop without further work. But most of the time, you will want to add smaller details to make the clouds more interesting. The best way to do this is to use Dons Brush to add additional opaque color in smaller round strokes, and then switch back to the Cloud brush and blend and refine these shapes. Figure 2.8 shows the lower-left side of the cloud bank where small opaque strokes were added over the first large layer of clouds. Figure 2.8 also shows how the small strokes have been blended and painted over using the Cloud brush in other areas of the cloud.

**Figure 2.8** Small, opaque colors are added in the lower left of the cloud for blending and adding more detail. Other sections of the clouds show how these small opaque strokes are blended into the underlying colors.

7. Create a new layer to add these smaller details. You do not want to work on the main Cloud layer in case it takes a few tries to get the look you want. It is much easier to experiment on a new layer and just delete the entire layer if it does not work the way you want. Make sure you have checked the Pick Up Underlying Color box in the Layers palette. Not checking the box can make the brushes behave in ways you may not want.

The edges of the cloud shapes against the sky are very crisp in some areas and need to be softened.

8. Choose Dons Blender, set Opacity to about 23%, and with a light touch, blend some of the harsher cloud edges into the surrounding sky colors. Figure 2.9 shows the results of blending the cloud edges into the surrounding sky.

9. If you have not done so already, save your image.

**Figure 2.9**  Using Dons Blender and a light touch, blend the harsh edges of the clouds into the surrounding sky color.

## Refining the Details

Be sure to save your work before finishing the clouds for this painting. You want to make sure that you have a saved version to fall back on in case your finishing touches take a bit of practice and experimentation. There is really no specific point at which the clouds are finished. Use a bit of care and restraint as you paint them. It's a fun process, and you can get lost adding smaller and smaller details. But too many small areas, and the overall impression of a cloud can be lost.

1.  The final step to painting the clouds involves blending the edges, adding small details and bits back into the clouds, adding a few small dark clouds in front of the large background cloud, and generally cleaning up the image.

2.  If there are multiple layers with clouds painted on each, you should collapse them into one layer, but do not drop them down onto the Canvas layer quite yet.

3.  Blend the sharp horizon line so it has a much softer appearance. Darken the top-right and -left corners of the sky to increase the contrast between the sky and the clouds.

### Softening the Clouds

We'll do one last tweak to the clouds, and then we'll be finished with the clouds.

1.  Duplicate the Cloud layer, and make sure the duplicate is the active layer.

2.  In the Effects menu, select Soften.

3.  Set the adjustment slider to 6.5 or whatever looks good in the preview window. Click OK.

4.  Set the Opacity setting of the softened layer to about 50%.

5.  Collapse the two Cloud layers together.

The softened Cloud layer adds a nice soft-focus feeling to the clouds while still allowing the smaller details on the layer below to be seen. Figure 2.10 shows the finished Cloud layer. When you are happy with how the painting looks, make sure to save it once again.

**Figure 2.10** The finished Cloud layer

## Painting the Water

Water is another one of those elements in a landscape that can give an artist fits. Like clouds, water moves and changes shape constantly. Also like clouds, it is often best to paint the impression of water instead of trying to paint the actual shapes of water that you observe.

Again, because we are not using any reference material, the technical accuracy of the reflections and such is not as important as convincing the viewers that they are looking at some painted water. Painting the water is a process that depends on other areas of the image being finished or close to finished. This process will take several steps and cannot be completed in one block of work dedicated to just painting the water. We will do the initial work now and then return later in the painting process to finish.

The first steps when painting the water are not nearly as intensive as painting the clouds. The work is more along the lines of pushing the correct button in the correct sequence to get the right effect. In this section, we'll use several Painter X features in sequence to easily create a basic water effect. Later, we'll paint on and over this layer as the painting progresses.

We want to create a reflection of the clouds that will immediately give the impression of water to the viewer. To do this, first duplicate the Cloud layer.

1. Access the Duplicate command either by right-clicking on the Cloud layer and selecting Duplicate or by selecting the Duplicate command in the Layers menu on the menu bar at the top of the screen.

2. With the Duplicate layer active, navigate to the Effects menu and select Orientation > Flip Vertical. Figure 2.11 shows the location of the Flip Vertical command in the Effects menu.

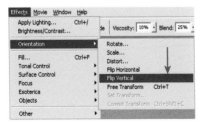

**Figure 2.11** The location of the Flip Vertical command

3. Once again, go to the Effects menu and select Orientation > Free Transform. Free Transform creates a Reference layer from the Duplicate Cloud layer that can be scaled, distorted, rotated, sheared, and generally changed to your heart's desire without ruining the original. The icon for the new Reference layer in the Layers palette is different from a normal layers icon. Figure 2.12 shows both a normal layer icon and the Reference layer icon.

 **Note:** It is important to remember the difference between the layer icon and the Reference layer icon, because you cannot paint on a Reference layer.

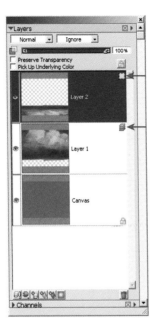

**Figure 2.12** The Layers palette showing both a normal layer and a Reference layer with their icons in the top-right corner of each layer

**4.** Scale down the Reference layer in the vertical dimension until the layer fills the painting from the horizon to the bottom of the image, and position it correctly along the bottom of the image.

We are trying to quickly create the base for a reflection of the clouds. Figure 2.13 shows the Cloud layer flipped, scaled down in the vertical axis, and positioned below the horizon line.

**Figure 2.13** The Duplicate Cloud layer is flipped, scaled, and moved into position below the horizon line to give the illusion of the clouds reflected in the water.

**5.** When you have finished transforming the Reference layer, you must convert it back to a default layer. To convert the Reference layer back to the normal layer, right-click on the layer and select Commit or, from the Effects menu, select Orientation > Commit Transform.

Now we need to make the reflected clouds look a bit more like water.

**6.** If it is not already visible, launch the Patterns palette. Click on the small black triangle in the upper-right corner of the palette. Then highlight Make Fractal Pattern from the pop-up menu. Figure 2.14 shows the location of the Make Fractal Pattern command in the Patterns palette.

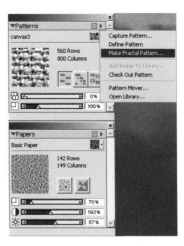

**Figure 2.14** The location of the Make Fractal Pattern menu item in the Patterns palette

7. The Make Fractal Pattern window appears. Set the sliders to the following values:

   - Power: −21%
   - Feature Size: 12%
   - Softness: 79%
   - Angle: 90
   - Thinness: 9%

   Then click 512 for the Size button.

8. Click OK. Figure 2.15 shows the Make Fractal Pattern window and the correct values for the sliders and Size button.

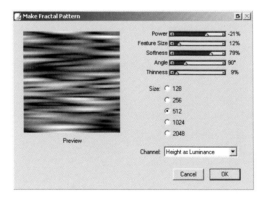

**Figure 2.15** The Make Fractal Pattern window with the correct values set in the sliders and checked in the buttons

A new image will be created with a seamless fractal pattern. *Seamless* in this case means that the edges of the image can be tiled or wrapped around on itself without a visible seam where one edge meets another. This image is going to be the base for creating a water-like effect in the reflected Cloud layer.

9. Once again in the Pattern palette, click on the small black triangle and highlight Capture Pattern. The Capture Pattern window appears. Leave all the settings at their default, but name the new pattern Water. Click OK to close the window.

**10.** Close the pattern image. Save it or just throw it away since we no longer need it in this painting.

**11.** Back in our main painting, make sure that the Cloud Reflection layer is active, and duplicate it so you have two Cloud Reflection layers. Click on the top Cloud Reflection layer to make it the active layer if it is not already, and click on the small plug icon at the bottom of the Layers palette to activate Dynamic Layers. Then select the Glass Distortion effect (see Figure 2.16).

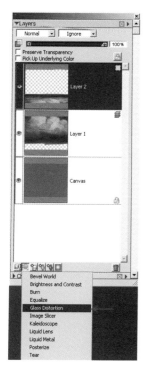

**Figure 2.16** Selecting the Glass Distortion Dynamic Layer

The Glass Distortion Options window appears, and the effect is applied to the current layer using the active Paper texture (Figure 2.17).

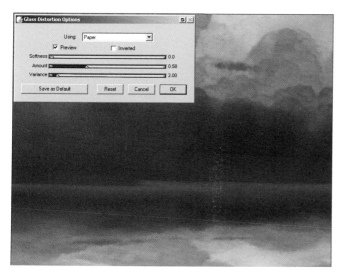

**Figure 2.17** The Glass Distortion Options window

Currently, the effect being applied is based on the active Paper texture. This texture obviously does not make the reflected clouds look like water.

**12.** To create a more convincing water effect, click the down triangle in the Using box and highlight Original Luminance.

**13.** Original Luminance points the effect to the currently active pattern to create the distortion. If the Water pattern created earlier is not the active pattern, go to the Patterns palette and select the Water pattern. Figure 2.18 shows the distortion switched from using Paper to Original Luminance with the Water pattern active.

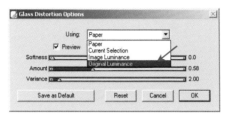

**Figure 2.18** The Glass Distortion effect using Original Luminance based on the earlier created Water pattern

The distortion in the cloud reflections is now looking a lot more like waves in water.

**14.** You can refine the effect with a few adjustments of the sliders. Move the sliders to the following values:

- Softness: 1.1
- Amount: 0.77
- Variance: 3.01

**15.** Also, in the Patterns palette, scale the pattern down to 65% of its original size. When you've made all the adjustments, click OK in the Options window (Figure 2.19).

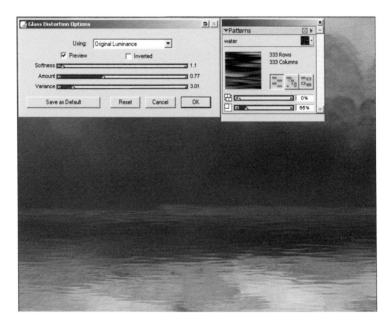

**Figure 2.19** The Glass Distortion Options slider settings, the Scaling slider in the Patterns palette, and the resulting change in the effect

One of the nice things about Dynamic Layers is the ability to adjust the effect at any time. As long as the layer has not been converted to a default layer, you can double-click on it, and the options box will open. Here you can experiment with different settings. When you are satisfied with the Dynamic Layer, you can convert it to a default layer by right-clicking on it in the Layers palette and selecting Commit. You can delete the first Reflection layer that is not distorted. Figure 2.20 shows the complete painting to this point.

**Figure 2.20**  The complete painting with cloud reflections in the foreground water

## Adding Perspective

The water is pretty convincing except that it does not recede into the distance as you would expect. It would be tedious, though possible, to make multiple layers that each had the watery effect applied slightly smaller. In this particular painting, I will opt for an easier solution. Instead of receding water, we will add a dark fog bank to cover the larger wave shapes as they get closer to the horizon line.

Follow these steps to create a dark fog bank.

1. Create a new layer. Make sure that the Preserve Transparency box is not checked and Pick Up Underlying Color box is checked.

2. Using the Dropper tool, select the darkest color that is close to the horizon. In the Color palette, make the selected color slightly darker.

3. Select the Brush tool and then the Airbrushes category. Choose the Digital Airbrush variant.

4. On the new layer, paint a slightly darker strip of color that covers the larger wave reflections that are close to the horizon line.

5. If the painted Foggy layer does not completely cover the reflections, duplicate the layer. Adjust the Opacity setting of the Duplicate layer until the reflections are hidden. Adjusting the opacity of a second layer gives much greater control than trying to paint additional color over the reflections.

6. The image now has four layers above the canvas background: two Fog layers, one Reflection layer, and the Cloud layer. Do not drop any layers yet. Save the file.

Figure 2.21 shows the painting with a foggy strip painted over the large reflections.

**Figure 2.21** The painting with a foggy strip painted over the large reflections in the water

### Dimming the Cloud Reflections

We have only one more step to take before we complete this stage of painting the water. The cloud reflections are a bit bright. Generally, reflections in water pick up some of the water color and are not as bright as the objects they reflect.

Follow these steps to make the reflections slightly less intense.

1. Create a new layer above the Reflection layer but below the Fog layers.

2. Create a rectangular selection from the horizon to the bottom of the image.

3. Fill the selection with a light bluish color.

4. Change the composite method of the layer to Darken. Setting a layer to Darken causes that layer to darken only the things that are lighter on the underlying layers.

5. Change the Opacity setting of the Darken layer to 50%.

Anything that was lighter on the Reflection layer has been subtly darkened and is slightly less intense. Figure 2.22 shows the painting with the water finished.

**Figure 2.22** The water in the painting is now finished as far as possible at this point.

Drop the Cloud layer onto the canvas and do an Iterative Save of the image again. For the rest of the painting, you do not need the clouds on a separate layer. Saving this new image with a new sequential number lets you go back to the original and access the Cloud layer if you need to.

In the next section, we will add rocky cliffs and outcroppings to the scene.

## Painting the Rocky Cliffs

The last major element to paint is stone. Now, stone *should* be easy to paint. It does not move or change shape in the time it takes to paint an image. On the other hand, because stones do not change, they are often hard to paint well because artists tend to assume they already know what rock looks like and they don't study it. The stones in this painting are not real but show one method of painting them.

We'll handle the rocks in this scene very simply and directly paint them on a new layer. No reference or preliminary sketches are being used. The sequence is similar to the way you would paint this subject matter in traditional media. Here are the basic steps:

1. Sketching the basic shapes of the rocks
2. Painting the colors of the rocks starting with dark colors and working toward light ones
3. Adding details and textures to the rocky surfaces
4. Cleaning up and finishing the painted rocks

We'll do the majority of the painting with Dons Brush, and we'll use a few additional default Painter brushes to add details. This part of the scene calls for multiple layers. From this point forward, check Pick Up Underlying Color for each new layer unless instructed differently.

To make sure that the perspective of the rocks is correct, turn on the perspective grid for the first sketches.

1. Turn the perspective grid on. You can find the command under the Canvas menu. Using the horizon line as the reference point, align the grid. The actual placing of the perspective grid is not critical. We'll use the grid as a guide to quickly draw a reference box. We'll sketch the rocks using the grid and box as guides. Figure 2.23 shows the perspective grid displayed over the painting. The horizon line is indicated by the black guideline, and the vanishing points are located where the horizontal and vertical guidelines cross.

**Figure 2.23** The perspective grid shown over the painting

2. Create a new layer and, using the grid and horizon line as guides, draw in a box that will be the basis for the future rocks. It's not important which brush you use. In this case, I used Dons Brush. Figure 2.24 shows the box shape sketched on the new layer.

3. Use Dons Brush to sketch some rocky shapes on a new layer inside the box. Fortunately, the rocks are randomly shaped, so their perspective does not have to be extremely accurate. Figure 2.25 shows the first of several rocks sketched within the box.

Figure 2.24 A box is sketched on a new layer as a guide for sketching in the cliffs and outcroppings.

Figure 2.25 A rock is sketched on a new layer inside the box.

This first rock is the most critical to set correctly in the painting, so that is why we used the perspective box. We will sketch the other rocks in relation to this first rock.

The first and most important of the rocks is drawn about one-third of the way across the horizontal space of the painting. This is good compositional practice because it keeps the image interesting to look at. We could have been placed it on either side of the image. Avoiding the central area for the focal point of a painting is always a good idea.

4.  Hide the perspective box and then paint dark colors into the shadow side of the rocks using Dons Brush. I have decided to add some house shapes on top of the rocks. I did this for two reasons: it adds interest to the painting, and it immediately gives a sense of scale to the rocky cliffs. Figure 2.26 shows the cliffs with darker shadows indicated and a roughly sketched series of buildings on the top faces.

**Figure 2.26** Shadows are painted and buildings are sketched on the tops of the cliffs.

5.  Using the same brush, paint additional rocks. Draw a long, thin bridge to span one set of rocks to the island buildings. Keep everything simple and subject to change. Add some lighter colors to the light sides of the rocks. Figure 2.27 shows the work at this point.

By this time, I pretty much have determined the direction of the painting. Quite a bit of work has been accomplished, but I am still using only one brush. I painted the rocks with lighter colors up high where the setting sun is lighting them, and I painted the lower areas in shadow using colors that relate to the darkest cloud colors.

6. Using the same brush in a smaller size, draw some cracks and features over the large painted rocky areas. Most of the basic shapes and colors are finished and ready to have details added (see Figure 2.28).

7. Add some bright red color to the areas where the shadows transition to the sunlit surfaces. These bright colors add interest and help separate the rocks from the clouds.

**Figure 2.27** More rocks and a bridge are added to the scene.

**Figure 2.28** Main colors are added along with some small defining details in the rocks. Everything is ready for the details and finishing touches.

### Adding Texture to the Rocks

You can quickly and easily add more detail in the rocks and bridge with a few simple steps.

1. Create a new layer.
2. Switch to the default Painter brush Chalk > Variable Chalk.
3. Pick the Cobblestone Paper texture from the book's paper library.
4. On the darker side of the rocks, using a color that is quite dark, paint in some rocky textures.
5. Change the paper to the small stone wall texture, and paint some texture on the bridge.

Because we added the texture on a new layer, we can simply erase all brush-strokes that spilled over into the sky or water areas.

We will add more textures as we continue painting the image. Follow the preceding steps when you paint the textures so clean-up is easy or so you can delete changes that do not look the way you hoped.

Figure 2.29 shows the painting with some brighter colors added to the rocky surfaces and some nice cobblestone textures painted into the shadow areas of the cliffs. We have done lots of work since the last image, and the painting is starting to look finished.

**Figure 2.29** Brighter colors have been added to the rocky surfaces, along with some nice textures in the shadow areas of the cliffs.

Collapse the Texture and Rock layers together and, using a combination of Dons Brush and the Variable Chalk brush, refine and integrate the textures into the rocky surface. Generally, I work from the dark colors to the light ones. Paint additional texture in both the light and dark rock surfaces. Use only a few different paper textures, but vary the scale of each texture frequently to make sure there is no monotony in the surface. Clean up the edges of the cliffs and buildings using the Eraser brush. Figure 2.30 shows the current state of the painting.

**Figure 2.30**  The painting after clean-up with Eraser

## Creating Pits and Holes

I want to add a few pits and holes to the rocky surface. Painting the effect with traditional media could be tedious. Fortunately, it is easy with Painter.

**1.**   Create a new layer.

**2.**   Choose the Variable Splatter brush variant in the Airbrushes Category, set it to a large size, and paint a number of dark spots over the surfaces of the rocks. Lots of small spots will end up in the background on top of the sky and water. Erase these stragglers.

**3.**   Duplicate the layer.

**4.**   Select the bottom layer, and check the Preserve Transparency box.

**5.** Switch brushes to Dons Brush or another of your choice. Pretty much any other brush will work.

**6.** Select a light color from the sunny side of the rocks, make it a bit lighter in the Colors palette, and paint over the spots on the bottom layer that are in the sunlit areas.

**7.** Select a color from the lighter area of the rocks in shadow, make it slightly lighter in the Colors palette, and paint over the spots in the lower shadow areas of the cliffs. Because the Preserve Transparency box is checked, nothing but the spots are affected.

**8.** Click the Layer Adjuster and, using the left and down keyboard arrows, slightly offset the lighter Spot layer under the darker spots.

**9.** Collapse the layers and erase any spots that are in the background.

It is quite amazing that something as simple as offsetting the layers gives the spots the appearance of pits and holes. Figure 2.31 shows the Spot layers painted over the cliffs and rocks.

**10.** To enhance the realism of the Spot layer, reduce its Opacity setting to around 50% or whatever value looks good. Collapse the Spot and Rock layers. The entire image is shown in Figure 2.32 after the Spot layer's opacity is reduced.

**Figure 2.31** The Spot layer painted over the cliffs and rocks

**Figure 2.32**  The Spot layer is reduced to an Opacity setting of 50%.

## Adding More Textural Effects

Let's add more textural effects to the rocks and cliffs.

1.  Create another new layer.

2.  Pick the Pixel Spray airbrush, use the Dropper tool to pick colors from around
    the image, and paint color specks onto the new layer.

    Figure 2.33 shows the results of using the Pixel Spray airbrush on a new layer.

**Figure 2.33**  The Pixel Spray airbrush is used to add more texture to the rocks.

3. Erase any stray pixels in the clouds or water.

4. Reduce the opacity of the layer to some value that looks good.

5. Collapse the Rock and Pixel Spray layers together.

6. Switch back to Dons Brush and repaint any cracks in the rocks that were covered by the Pixel Spray or spots. Select lighter colors from either the shadow rocks or the sunlit rocks, and paint edges along the cracks to give them a three-dimensional (3D) feel. Figure 2.34 shows the rocks and cliffs after repainting the cracks.

**Figure 2.34** The cracks are repainted and the cliffs are almost finished.

The rocks and cliffs are about 90 percent finished at this point, but something looks a bit off. The cliffs are not reflecting in the water yet, and we need to fix this. In the next section, we will revisit the water and create the reflections.

## Completing the Water

Well, it is back to the water to paint the reflections of the cliffs. The process is essentially identical to the earlier steps we used to paint the reflections of the clouds.

1. To create the reflection, we first must duplicate the Rock layer, flip the layer vertically, transform it slightly in the vertical dimension, and position it under the main Cliff layer. Figure 2.35 shows how the Duplicate Cliff layer has been positioned under the main Cliff layer.

2. Duplicate the Cliff Reflection layer. Convert the Duplicate layer to a Dynamic Layer using the Glass Distortion effect. Use Original Luminance and the Water pattern as the driving texture for the Dynamic Layer. The reflection takes on a wavy appearance similar to the cloud reflections.

**Figure 2.35** The Cliff layer is duplicated. The duplicate is transformed and positioned under the original.

**3.** Convert the Dynamic Layer to a default layer.

**4.** Delete the original Cliff Reflection layer. Figure 2.36 shows the reflections of the cliffs now in place.

**Figure 2.36** The Dynamic Layer effect has been applied to the Cliff Reflection layer.

We need to clean up and paint over several rough edges and white spots to finish the Reflection layer. Also, we need to darken the Rock Reflection layer a bit, as it has the same value as the cliffs.

5. Duplicate the Reflection layer. Select the top Duplicate Reflection layer, and change the composite method to Multiply. The layer is now very dark with too much contrast.

6. Reduce the opacity of the dark layer until the combined appearance of the two is slightly darker than the cliffs.

7. Collapse the two layers together. Figure 2.37 shows the result of darkening the Cliff Reflection layer.

**Figure 2.37** The Cliff Reflection layer is darkened slightly.

Now all we need to do to finish the water is to clean up the waves, paint the area where the water meets the rock surfaces, and add a few highlights to the water surface.

8. Create a new layer to make fixing any mistakes easier.

9. Pick Dons Brush, and paint all the little reflections and corrections in the wave's surfaces. Figure 2.38 shows the small highlights and reflections added to the reflected water.

10. When you are done with all your corrections and finishing work, select all the layers and collapse them together.

We will now have one layer above the Canvas layer with the clouds painted on it. The painting is almost done. In the next section, we will add the finishing touches to the small buildings on the top of the rocks and anywhere else that final touches are needed.

**Figure 2.38** The Water layer is finished with small highlights.

## Finishing Touches

The painting is just about complete. The only thing left to do is paint some detail into the small buildings perched on the cliff tops.

At the last moment, I decide that the cliffs and buildings are too dull and do not look like they are being lit in a sunset. This is easy to correct even at this late stage in the painting.

Follow these steps to make the buildings and cliffs more colorful.

1. Duplicate the Cliff layer.

2. With the top Duplicate layer active, select Adjust Colors from the Effects > Tonal Control menu and increase the Saturation setting until the orange color on the buildings is much brighter in the preview window. The blues will also become intense, but that is not a problem. When the saturation is to your liking, click OK.

3. Select the Eraser tool and carefully erase the bright blue shadow areas on the top layer to reveal the underlying cliffs.

4. Be careful as you erase into the transition areas between the bright sunlight and bluish shadows. Leave some of the bright colors found on this edge for visual interest. Figure 2.39 shows a close-up of the transition edge between the orange

sunlit portions of the cliff and the shadows. Note the bright red and purple colors that have been left in some areas.

Save the image again. Now the cliffs and buildings look much more like they are being lit by the setting sun. Figure 2.40 shows the complete painting.

**Figure 2.39** Notice the bright red and purple colors.

**Figure 2.40** The entire painting after the light on the cliffs and buildings has been adjusted

Finally, we will add some small details to the buildings, drop all the layers to the canvas, copy and paste the whole image back onto itself, and add a lighting effect.

Because the buildings are so small, there is no need for lots of small details.

1. Create a new layer and, using Dons Brush, create a hint of sideboards, add some windows, paint in a few lightning rods, and add a top surface to the bridge.

2. When the results are satisfactory, drop all the layers onto the canvas. Figure 2.41 shows the painting with some detail added to the buildings.

**Figure 2.41** Some detail has been added to the buildings on top of the cliffs.

3. Select the whole painting, copy it, and paste it back onto itself.

4. Click on the top layer to make it active if it is not already, and select Apply Lighting from the Effects > Surface Control menu. Select the lighting variation Plain Light, and click OK.

5. Reduce the Opacity setting of the layer with the new lighting effect to 30%. Reducing the opacity softens the effect until it adds that small extra touch to the whole painting.

The painting is finally finished (Figure 2.42).

**Figure 2.42** The finished painting

## Final Thoughts

This has been a large tutorial covering a lot of material. You have learned how to paint large and fluffy clouds using only a few simple brushes, create a reflection of the clouds that looks like water, paint some cliffs and stones using several techniques to make the process faster, paint in finishing touches, and add a subtle lighting effect to bring the painting to life.

As with everything else in this book, the techniques in this chapter will not replace good painting and drawing skills. These techniques do not make a work of art and cannot be relied on to rescue a bad painting. Continue to practice your drawing and painting skills, and these techniques will quickly help you produce a better painting.

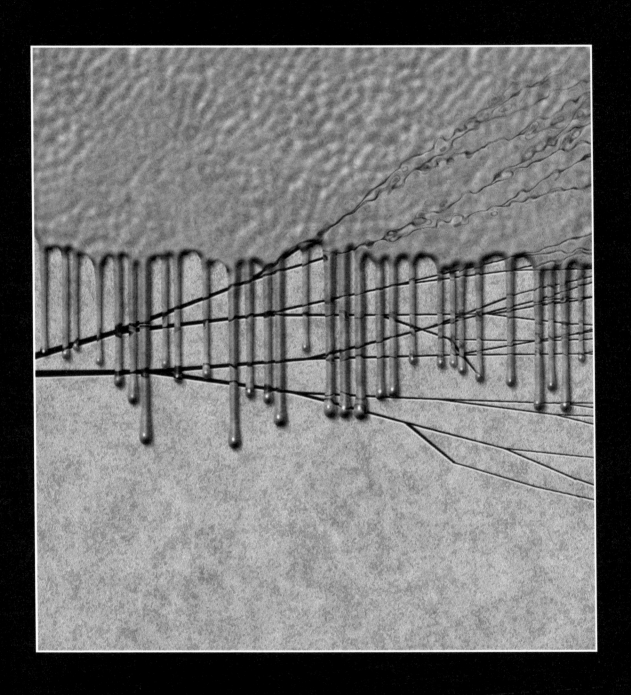

# Painting a Rocky Surface Then Making It Look Wet

*This chapter shows you how to use Painter to create several effects.*

*We will start off using several features in painter that make it easy to create a rocky looking texture. This texture will be used as the base for two smaller tutorials about creating or painting different wet-looking effects that will be useful in your Painter arsenal as you work on your own digital paintings.*

*You will learn how to use several new tools as you work through the tutorials in this chapter. These tools include the various effects in the Effects menu, the Dynamic Plug-ins, different Composite Methods on layers, the Create Fractal Pattern menu, and Gradients.*

3

**Chapter Contents**

## Creating a Rocky Texture

This section explores some of Painter's features so you can create a realistic-looking rocky texture. You can expand on these basic steps to create a limitless supply of natural-looking rocky textures.

Let's begin by using the Create Fractal Pattern Command.

Because the menu items that we need to make our texture are available only when an image is open or a new image is created, we will make an image to work with first. After we create the image, we can minimize it to get it out of the way.

**1.** Create a new image. It does not matter what the size of the image is, because you will not use it.

The rocky texture we will create is based on the Make Fractal Pattern command. This command creates a new image.

**2.** Select Make Fractal Pattern in the Patterns palette, and an options box opens. The options box opens and looks like Figure 3.1.

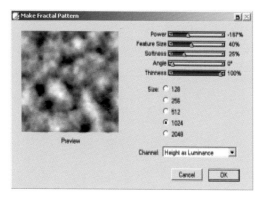

**Figure 3.1** The Make Fractal Pattern options box

We will make our texture by layering several fractal patterns. Each pattern is individually created using various settings in this box. We can achieve the best results by creating at least four individual fractal patterns. Of course, we can use more. The number of fractal patterns that are layered to create the rocky texture is limited only by our patience and creativity.

It is usually best to start with large patterns on the bottom layers and cover them with smaller patterns on the upper layers. Experiment, though, since something as simple as changing the order of the fractal layers will produce completely different textures.

Another nice attribute of the patterns we create with the Fractal Pattern command is that the patterns themselves are seamless. The edges can wrap around on themselves, and there is no visible line where they join. This feature is important if we are going to make paper textures or if we will be using these textures in three-dimensional (3D) programs.

3. Use the following settings for the Make Fractal Pattern by adjusting the sliders and buttons:

- Power: –167%
- Feature Size: 40%
- Softness: 25%
- Angle: 0
- Thinness: 100%
- Size: Select the 1024 button
- Leave the channel box set to Height as Luminance

These settings will give you a pattern made of fairly large shapes. You will use this pattern as the base for the rest of the image.

After you change your settings, the preview also changes. Unfortunately, this preview gives you only a general idea of the size of the light and dark shapes; it does not really reflect the look of the pattern when it is applied to a large image.

4. When you are finished, click OK. A new image is created that is 1024 pixels in both the vertical and horizontal dimensions and will look something like Figure 3.2.

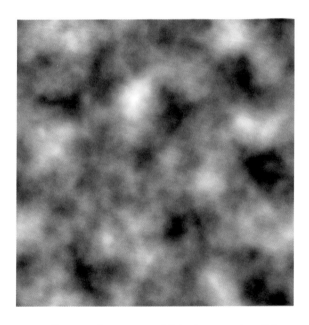

**Figure 3.2** A pattern created using the Make Fractal Pattern command from within the Patterns menu

5. Repeat the process. This time set the sliders to the following settings:

- Power: –167%
- Feature Size: 92%
- Softness: 0°
- Angle: 0%
- Thinness: 100%

The 1024 size button should already be selected from the earlier pattern, but if it is not, select it. Click OK when you are finished.

The pattern generated should look like Figure 3.3 and will be made of larger shapes.

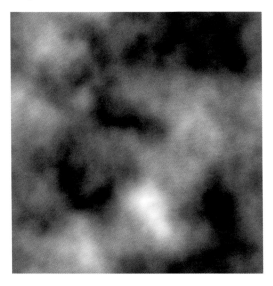

**Figure 3.3** The second fractal pattern with larger shapes

Patterns made of large soft shapes like these last two are generally said to contain low-frequency noise. Patterns made of lots of little shapes are said to contain high-frequency noise.

6. Create another pattern using the following settings:

- Power: –227%
- Feature Size: 19%
- Softness: 0
- Angle: 0
- Thinness: 100%

This pattern is made of smaller but still generally soft shapes. Your pattern should look something like Figure 3.4.

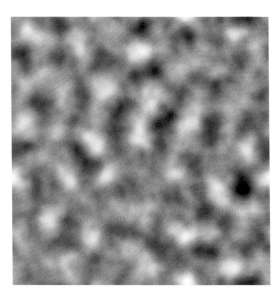

**Figure 3.4** The third fractal pattern

Finally, we will create two patterns that consist of high-frequency noise.

7. Use the following settings for the first pattern:
   - Power: –45%
   - Feature Size: 56%
   - Softness: 1
   - Angle: 0
   - Thinness: 100%

   Click OK, and you will have a new image that looks something like Figure 3.5.

**Figure 3.5** A fractal pattern with high-frequency noise

8. And use the following settings for the second pattern:
   - Power: –45%
   - Feature Size: 31%
   - Softness: 55
   - Angle: 0
   - Thinness: 100%

   Click OK, and a new image will be created that looks similar to Figure 3.6.

   You don't need to use the exact settings described in the tutorial; they are given as a starting point. Feel free to experiment with different settings.

   We will layer these five individual images into one image to create a natural stony texture. Before combining them into one image, we need to add some color to them. This is easy to do in Painter using gradients.

Figure 3.6 The last fractal pattern that
will be used to create the stony texture

## Adding Color Using Gradients

Several default gradients are available in the Gradients palette, and we can use any of
them. For this tutorial, though, we want to choose something that has earthy colors.

We can edit any of the gradients for this tutorial, but it is often easiest to start
with the simplest.

1.  Open the Gradients palette if it is not already visible. Then select the Two-Point
    gradient from the available default library. The gradient preview updates imme-
    diately with a gradient made from the primary and secondly colors currently
    active in the Colors palette.

    We want to change the primary and secondary colors to something more rock-
    like. Tans and grays would be a good combination to start with.

2.  In the Gradients palette, click on the small triangle in the upper-right corner
    and select Edit Gradient. The Edit Gradient box appears with a linear gradient
    displayed.

3.  Editing this gradient is quite easy. Click anywhere in the displayed gradient,
    and a small arrow point appears along the bottom edge of the display. Click in
    the Colors palette to assign a new color to this point. Continue adding colors
    until you have something that looks like Figure 3.7.

Figure 3.7 The Edit Gradient box

You can change any of the gradient colors at any time. Simply reselect the small arrow point and then choose a new color from the Colors palette. If you end up with too many colors and want to eliminate a few, just select the applicable arrow point and press the Backspace key.

It is generally a good idea to make the first and last color in the gradient the same color. Doing so makes the transition between colors smoother in the next step when you color the five patterns.

**4.** When the gradient looks the way you want, click OK. It is now active and displayed in the Gradients palette. It is a good idea to save the custom gradient just in case there is a problem and you need to access it in the future. Use the Gradient Mover to save the custom gradient.

**Note:** The gradient used in this tutorial is available for download.

Coloring the textures using our edited gradient is the easiest part of the entire process.

**5.** Select one of the textures created earlier to start off. With the custom gradient active, highlight Express In Image from the Gradients drop-down menu in the upper-right corner of the Gradients palette. Figure 3.8 shows the location of this command.

**6.** The Express In Image options box appears with only one control: the Bias slider. Use the Bias slider shown in Figure 3.9 to cycle through the colors of the gradient in the textured image.

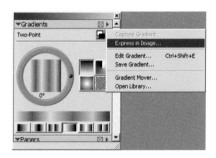

**Figure 3.8** The location of the Express in Image command

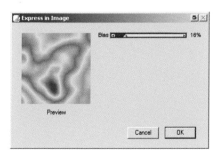

**Figure 3.9** Moving the Bias slider changes how the gradient is mapped into the pattern.

All the colors in the gradient will be used; the Bias slider just shows how the colors are mapped into the image. There is no right or wrong setting, so experiment with different Bias settings.

7. Click the OK button, and the gradient will be mapped into the texture created earlier and look something like Figure 3.10.

Apply the same gradient to each of the remaining four images. Figures 3.11 to 3.14 show each image with the same gradient mapped into it.

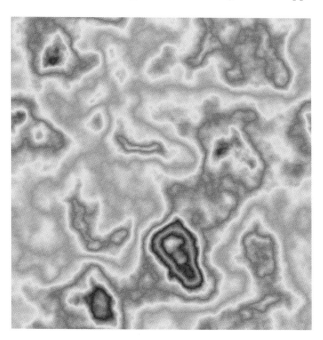

**Figure 3.10** The first pattern with the gradient mapped into it

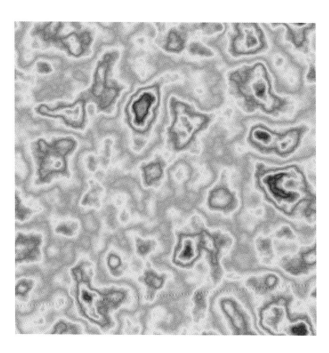

**Figure 3.11** The second pattern with the gradient mapped into it

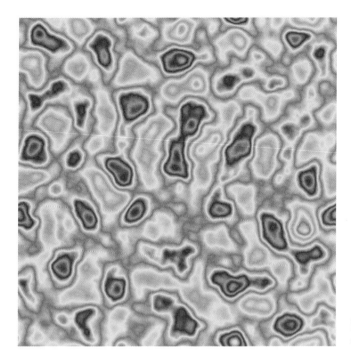

**Figure 3.12** The third pattern
with the gradient mapped into it

**Figure 3.13** The fourth pattern
with the gradient mapped into it

As the frequency of the noise in the image gets higher, the size of the individual colored shapes becomes smaller until the final image has an almost sandy appearance, like Figure 3.14.

**Figure 3.14** This pattern has a sand-like appearance.

It does not matter if the images you have created do not look just like the example images. The method of creating these images in Painter is what is important, not duplicating my results.

All we need to do now is to combine all five of the individual images into one rocky-looking texture.

## Combining the Images into One Texture

Right now, none of the individual textured images look much like a rock. In this next section, we will combine the textures into one image that will have a more realistic look and feel of rock.

1.  Select the texture with the largest colored shapes to use as the base of the image.

2.  Copy and paste each of the remaining four images into this first image. Put the textures with the largest colored shapes on the bottom layers and those with the smallest sandy textures on the top.

3.  The real work begins now as you lower the Opacity setting of each layer to around 50 percent. Evaluate the appearance of the entire image, and then rearrange the layers to see many different looks. Figure 3.15 shows the Layers palette with the five layers and, in this case, the top and second layer switched.

Each layer is at 50 percent opacity in the default Composite Method. Figure 3.16 shows the whole image with a convincing rocky appearance.

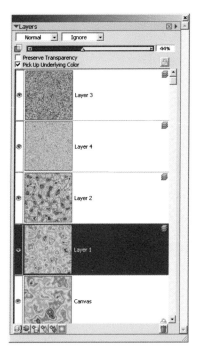

**Figure 3.15** The Layers palette with the five layers visible

**Figure 3.16** The image now has a very rock-like appearance.

Lest you think your options are limited when rearranging the layers, you should know that if you only rearrange five layers with no additional changes to any of them, you will have created a total of 120 different textures. When you start to make changes to any or all layers, the possibilities are virtually endless.

The last touch is to add a small bit of 3D texture to the surface of the rock.

4. From the Effects menu, select Surface Control > Apply Surface Texture. The Apply Surface Texture options box appears (Figure 3.17). Numerous settings and controls are available in this box.

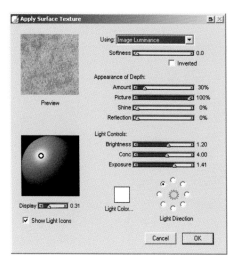

**Figure 3.17**  The Apply Surface Texture options box

5. Watch the preview window update as you change the default options to the following:

- Change the Using menu from Paper to Image Luminance. This designates the light and dark passages in the image to drive the 3D effect instead of the active paper texture.

- Set the Amount to about 30%. The Amount of the effect applied is much more effective when it is set to a lower value than a higher one.

- Reduce the Shine slider to 0%. We don't need or want a shiny surface.

Leave the rest of the settings at their default value and click OK. A nice subtle rough surface is added to the rock, finishing the image. Figure 3.18 shows the results.

**Figure 3.18**  The rocky image after applying a surface texture

Now you know a process for creating realistic-looking rock textures. With this knowledge, you can create an infinite number of variations. This is only the beginning. As you become more familiar with the many features of Painter X, your creative options will continue to expand.

In the following tutorials, we will use this texture as the base for some interesting painting effects.

## Painting a Wet Surface

In this tutorial, we will take the rock texture created earlier and paint a wet surface on it. Creating a surface that looks wet is not difficult. In fact, it is much easier in Painter than it would be with traditional media.

Once the wet surface is painted, we will vary the method slightly to create an additional wet-looking surface with different characteristics.

Open the rocky texture that you created in the earlier tutorial if it is not open already. The following steps are simple to follow and do not need in-depth explanation.

1. Create a new layer, and make sure that Pick Up Underlying Color is selected and Preserve Transparency is not. Name the layer Wet.

2. Using the Rectangular Selection tool, drag a rectangular marquee around the top third or so of the new layer.

3. Using the Paint Bucket, fill the selection with a mid-value gray.

4. Select a brush of your choice, and paint a series of drips and runs using the gray that is already on the layer. While the brush you choose is really not important, the Smooth Ink variant in the Pens category works nicely. Figure 3.19 shows the new gray layer painted over the rocky base.

**Figure 3.19** The gray drips painted on a new layer

## Duplicating for Future Use

**1.** In future steps, you will need a selection created from the Wet layer so, in the Layers menu, with the Wet layer active, select Load Selection. When the Options box appears, leave the default settings as they are and click OK. A new selection is drawn around the drips.

**2.** Save the selection. The Save Selection command is found in the Select menu. There is not a keyboard shortcut for this command.

**3.** Deselect the layer using Ctrl+D (⌘+D on the Mac).

**4.** Change the Composite Method of the Dripping layer to Multiply. The layer now begins to look like wetness on top of the rock (Figure 3.20).

**5.** Duplicate the Wet layer and hide the duplicate by clicking on the small eye icon. The duplicate is created just in case you make any mistakes. You can then easily correct them by reverting to the original Wet layer. In most cases, you will delete this duplicate layer at the end of the painting.

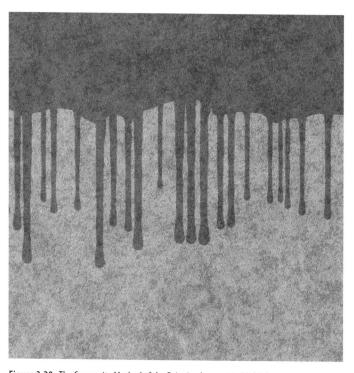

**Figure 3.20** The Composite Method of the Dripping layer set to Multiply

While the Wet layer is starting to look wet, it is rather flat and unconvincing. We need to do some additional work and add a few details to give some depth and dimension to the drips. Some details that would make the drips more realistic would be shadows, highlights on the drips themselves, some darker areas on the drips, and some lighter colors where the light is concentrated as it shines through the liquid.

We can perform the different steps to add the details in any order, but first we will create some shadows for the drips and add highlights and finishing touches.

## Creating Shadows

1. Load the selection made from the drips.

2. With the Canvas layer selected, copy and paste in place a new layer that is made out of the rocky canvas. Name the new layer `Rocky Drip`.

3. With the new layer active, select Create Drop Shadow from the Effects menu, Objects submenu.

4. Leave the settings at their defaults except the Collapse to One Layer box. If it is selected, deselect it. If it is not selected, leave it as is. Click OK. Figure 3.21 shows the Drop Shadow options box.

A new layer group is created that contains both the rocky drips and the drop shadow. The image looks something like Figure 3.22.

**Figure 3.21** The Drop Shadow options box

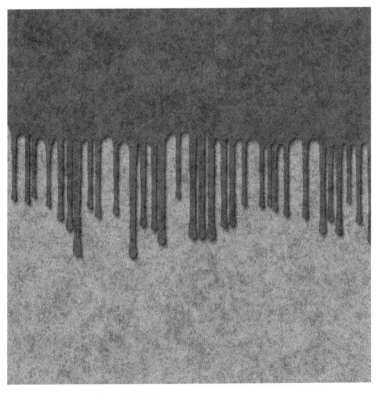

**Figure 3.22** A drop shadow added to the image

Why did we need to create a new rocky layer to produce the drop shadow? Why not just use the original drip layer that makes the surface look wet? The problem lies in the wet-looking layer. Applying a drop shadow to any layer creates a dark shadow under that entire layer. Because the Composite Method of the Wet layer is set to Multiply, you can see through this layer. The entire Shadow layer would be visible through the Multiply layer, creating a dark image and not successfully creating a drop shadow effect.

5.  Ungroup the Shadow and Rocky Drip layers using the Ungroup command in the Layers menu, or use the keyboard shortcut Ctrl+U (⌘+U on the Mac).

6.  With the Shadow layer active, use the Eraser tool to carefully erase some of the shadow at the tops of the drips. The thickness of the wet area is less at the top and greater at the actual drips, so a smaller and less distinct shadow is appropriate. Figure 3.23 shows the image with some of the higher shadows erased.

The drop shadow is now finished.

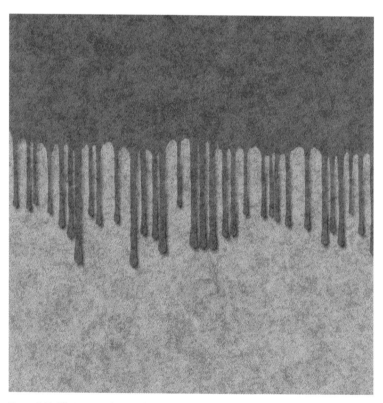

**Figure 3.23** The image with some of the higher shadow areas erased

### Adding Shine

Now we will add a bit of shine to the Rocky Drip layer using the Apply Surface Texture command.

1.  With the Rocky Drip layer active, select Apply Surface Texture from the Effects menu, Surface Control submenu.

2. The options box appears. Change the Using menu to Image Luminance, the Amount to about 50%, and the Shine slider to 100%. Then click OK (Figure 3.24).

The Rocky Drip layer now has a nice subtle shine, as you can see in Figure 3.25.

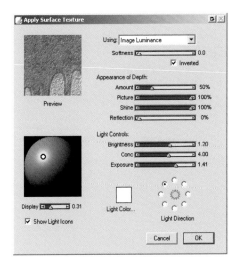

**Figure 3.24** The Apply Surface Texture options box

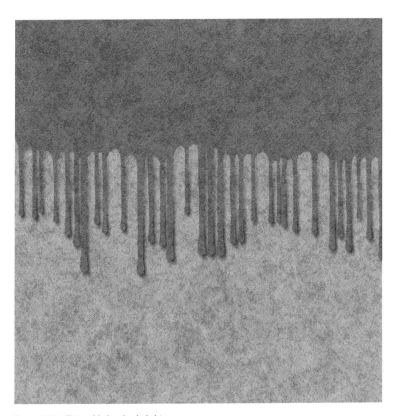

**Figure 3.25** Shine added to the dark drips

## Darkening and Softening

All we have left to do is to add some finishing touches to the drips.

1. Create a new layer on which to paint the dark side of the drips.

2. Load the drips selection.

3. Using the Digital Airbrush, paint some dark areas on the left side of the drips. Do not paint the darks too opaque and dark.

4. Change the Composite Method of the layer to Multiply.

5. Lower the Opacity setting of the layer to a percentage where you can see the underlying Rock layer.

6. In the Effects menu, select Focus > Soften, and set the Amount to 5.

   The dark sides of the drips are painted and look like Figure 3.26.

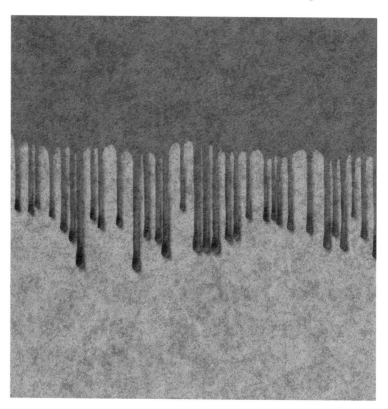

**Figure 3.26** Darker areas are painted into the drips.

## Adding Reflected Light

We will now paint light reflecting inside the drip.

1. Create a new layer and reload the drip selection.

2. Using Dons brush or another brush of your choice, carefully paint the reflected light on the lower-right side of each drip using one of the lightest rock colors.

3. Soften the painted edges slightly.

4. Change the Composite Method of the layer to Overlay.

5. In the Select menu, pick None and, of course, save the image.

The drips now look more 3D, as in Figure 3.27.

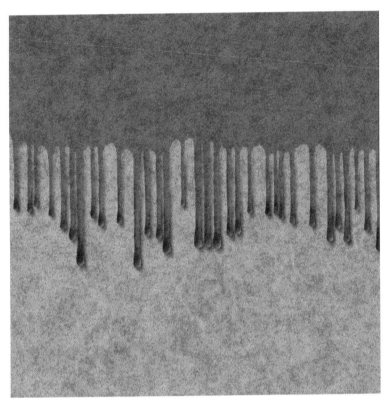

**Figure 3.27** Lighter reflections are added to the drips.

## Adding Highlights

The final touch will be to add some highlights to the drips.

1. Create one more new layer.

2. Using Dons brush or any other brush of your choice, paint a bright highlight in the darkest areas on each drip. The highlight should be fairly crisp without much softening.

3. Select the Glow brush, which you can find in the FX category of brushes.

4. Pick a rather bright orange color, and lightly paint on each highlight. The Glow brush gives a subtle orange edge to each highlight.

The highlights are in place (Figure 3.28).

You can drop all the layers onto the canvas, create a clone image, or just save the layered image, depending on your ultimate use.

The painting is finished. You can see that painting a wet surface is not that difficult in Painter X.

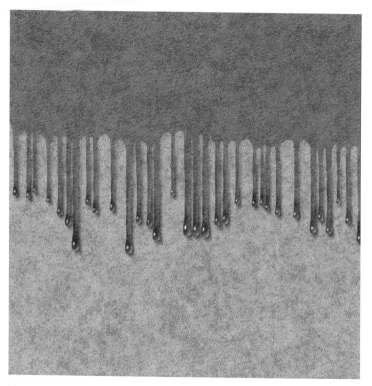

**Figure 3.28** Highlights in the drips

In the next section and using the same approach, we will create another wet-looking surface, but this time we will give it a rather gooey appearance. The effect is similar to what it would look like if we dribbled oil over the surface instead of water.

## Painting a Gooey Surface

In this section, we will paint a wet effect that looks a lot more viscous, thick, and gooey. Many of the steps are identical to the previous tutorial and will not be repeated in depth again.

We'll start out by using the same texture image and Drip layer that we created in the previous tutorial.

Because the texture we are using has no large repeating areas, it would normally be hard to see some of the distortions that this technique produces. To make the effect more successful, we will add some cracks to the rocky surface. We can either draw cracks on a new layer or, in this case, use another of Painter's features, Growth, to create some crack-like shapes.

### Creating Cracks in the Rocks

1. Create a new layer, and make sure that the Preserve Transparency box is not selected. Name the layer Cracks.

2. Select a darker color from the image. In the Color palette, make the selected color dark.

3. With this new layer active, select Esoterica > Growth from the Effects menu.

4. The Growth options box appears and displays a number of sliders and a preview window (Figure 3.29).

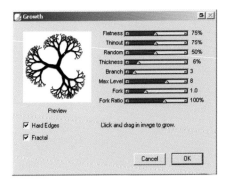

**Figure 3.29** The Growth options box

Growth is a rather strange effect that makes plant-like designs. The actual use of the effect is limited only by your imagination.

5. To make the tree shapes look more like a crack, move the sliders to the following settings:
   - Flatness: 89%
   - Thinout: 53%
   - Random: 100%
   - Thickness: 2%
   - Branch: 1
   - Max Level: 6
   - Fork: .5
   - Fork Ratio: 105%

The options box with the sliders set to the correct settings is shown in Figure 3.30.

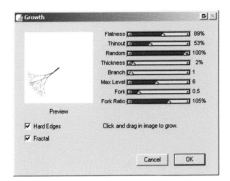

**Figure 3.30** The settings to use in the Growth box

Of course, you are encouraged to experiment with other settings. The settings suggested will work for this project, but there are many others that would work well, too.

6. With the Growth options box still open, use your stylus to click and drag in the image from the center of the image out.

7. A circle will appear as you drag, showing the extent of the growth being created. When the circle takes up most of the image, let up on the stylus, and a new growth will be created. The image will look something like Figure 3.31.

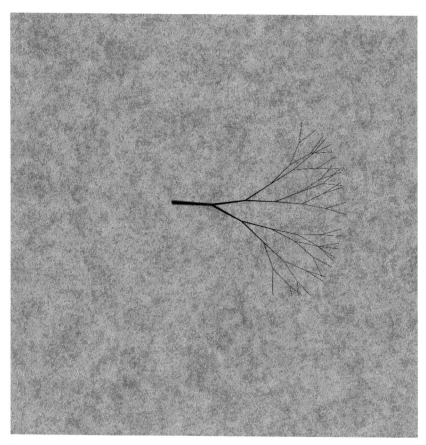

**Figure 3.31** The growth results on a new layer

The orientation of the growth in your image will probably be different. This is not a problem, since you will be adjusting both the size and direction of the growth to make it look more like cracks.

8. From the Effects menu, select Orientation > Free Transform.

9. Rotate and scale the Growth layer until it extends off the edges of the image, lies in a horizontal direction, and generally looks more like cracks in the rock. The image will look something like Figure 3.32.

10. When the layer is in position, finalize the transform by right-clicking the layer and selecting Commit.

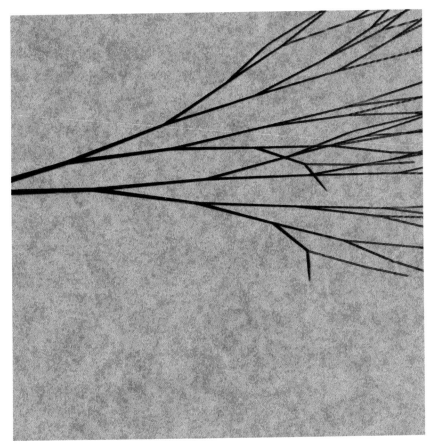

**Figure 3.32** The Growth layer is rotated, scaled, and moved into place.

## Giving the Cracks Dimension

1. Duplicate the layer.

2. Click the bottom Crack layer and check the Preserve Transparency box at the top of the Layers palette.

3. Using a brush with a high Opacity setting, select one of the lightest colors in the rocky surface and paint the cracks. Because the Preserve Transparency box is selected, only the cracks will be painted.

   There are now two layers: one that is dark, and beneath it one that is identical but lighter in color.

4. Click the eye on the top Crack layer to make it visible again.

5. Activate the Layer Adjuster tool in the toolbox. Using the arrow keys to move the lighter Crack layer, slightly offset it beneath and to the right of the darker Crack layer. The image will now look something like Figure 3.33.

6. Select both Crack layers, and collapse them into one layer.

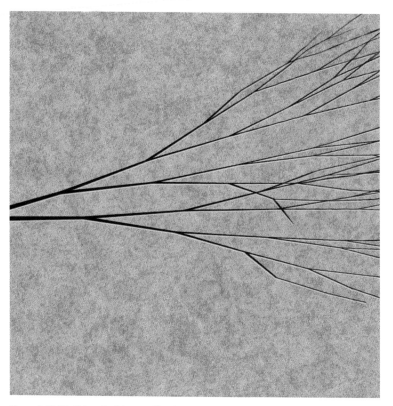

**Figure 3.33**  The lighter Crack layer is offset slightly below and to the right of the darker cracks.

The actual realistic look of the cracks is not important. You can paint them by hand if you want a different look. What is important is that there is now an element that will help display the distortion of the wet and gooey look that we are about to create.

Before we actually create the wet and gooey look, we need to create a new layer that has our cracked stone in it.

**1.**  Drop the Crack layer onto the background rock image.

**2.**  Load a selection using the Drip layer.

**3.**  Copy and Paste In Place the Canvas layer with the cracks. Name the layer something like `Rock Drips`.

There should now be three layers: the Drip layer, the Rock Drips layer with bits of the rock cracks running through it, and the Canvas layer that has the rocky surface and cracks.

## Getting Gooey

Now, to create the wet look but with a nice gooey and thick feeling, follow these steps:

**1.**  With the Rock Drips layer active, navigate to the Effects menu and select Focus > Glass Distortion.

**2.**  The Glass Distortion Options box opens (Figure 3.34).

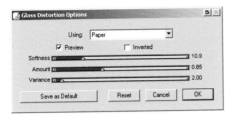

**Figure 3.34** The Glass Distortion Options box

3.  Use Paper as the driving texture, and set the sliders to the following values:
    - Softness: 10.9
    - Amount: 0.85
    - Variance: 2.00

4.  If you do not see a significant amount of distortion in the preview window, try changing the paper texture. Larger patterned textures give the best results.

5.  When the preview shows results that are acceptable, click OK.

A rippled, curved effect is applied to the new layer. You can see the results in Figure 3.35.

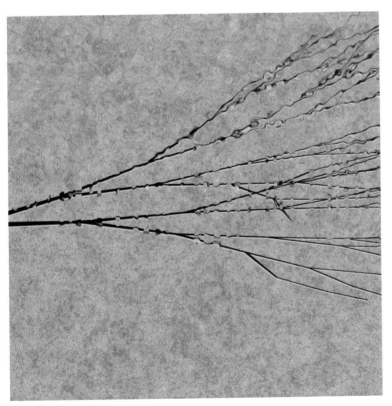

**Figure 3.35** Glass distortion is applied to the Drip layer.

The reason for creating the cracks in the stone now becomes quite clear. In the background rocky surface, you can see the glass distortion effect, but it is somewhat subtle. With the added cracks, you can see exactly what has happened to the surface.

## Adding Dimension

The drips have been distorted, but they have no dimension. Instead of manually adding a darker layer and painting shadows and highlights, we will use Dynamic Plug-ins to accomplish basically the same thing. Dynamic Plug-ins create dynamic layers and are a great feature to add to your creative arsenal in Painter X.

You can completely modify the effects of each dynamic layer at any time and any number of times without changing the source image. To create a dynamic layer, you use the Dynamic Plug-ins button located at the bottom of the Layers palette. By clicking the button at the bottom of the Layers palette that has an electrical plug as its icon, you create a Dynamic layer with one of 11 different effects.

1. Click the Dynamic Plug-ins button and, from the dialog box that pops up, choose Bevel World.

2. The Bevel World options box appears with a large number of sliders and settings (Figure 3.36).

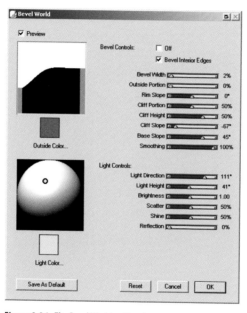

**Figure 3.36** The Bevel World options box

3. Set the sliders to the following amounts:
   - Bevel Width: 2%
   - Outside Portion: 0
   - Rim Slope: 0°
   - Cliff Portion: 50%
   - Cliff Height: 50%
   - Cliff Slope: 67°
   - Base Slope: 45°
   - Smoothing: 100%
   - Light Direction: 111°

- Light Height: 41°
- Brightness: 1.00
- Scatter: 50%
- Shine: 50%
- Reflection: 0%

4. Change the Light Color to a warm light tan color by clicking on the color box.

5. When you are finished making the changes, click OK.

The distorted Drip layer now has a three-dimensional feeling without a lot of hand painting (Figure 3.37).

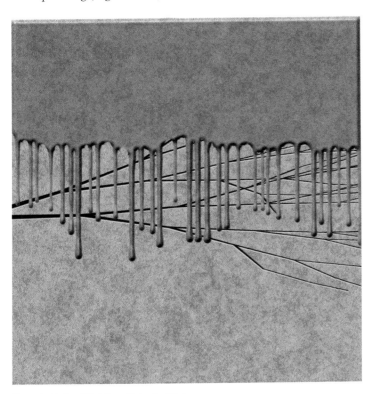

**Figure 3.37** Bevel World is applied to the Drip layer.

If the settings do not work the way you expected, you can double-click on the Dynamic layer and experiment with different settings.

When you are satisfied with the look of the Drip layer, right-click on it and Commit the layer. This turns a Dynamic layer into a regular layer that can be edited like any other.

## Removing the Bevel

You may have noticed that there is a large bevel around the top and sides of the Drip layer. You may or may not want this. In this case, I do not want the beveled edges.

Removing them is simple. Just follow these steps to remove the bevel along the top and left edges:

1. Drag a long, horizontal rectangular selection across the image somewhere below the beveled top edge.

2. Feather the selection. The default setting of 3 is fine.

3. Copy and paste the selected portion of the layer.

4. Move up the new layer so that it covers the bevel at the top of the image. Figure 3.38 shows some of the top bevel covered.

5. Repeat the procedure for the left bevel, except use a long, vertical, rectangular selection.

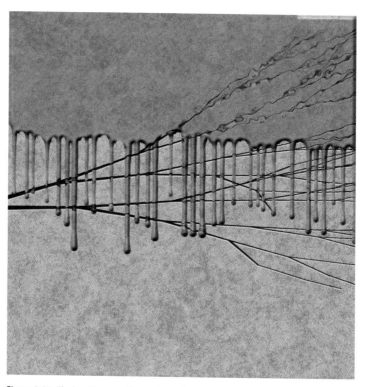

**Figure 3.38** The bevel is covered by copying and pasting selections from within the Drip layer.

Because the bevel on the right side of the image has lots of cracks, you cannot copy and paste a large section from another place in the image and have it work. The solution is to use a cloning brush and carefully paint around the cracks.

6. Choose the Soft Cloner brush. It is a variant in the Cloners brush category. Carefully paint out the bevel on the left side of the Drip layer using the Soft Cloner brush.

There are only a few things left to do to complete the painting. The drops still need a shadow. A strong highlight will help the drips look wet. Some additional texture added to the overall Drip layer is needed to remove the flat appearance of the Drip layer.

## Adding More Shadows, Highlights, and Texture

The first thing to do is add a shadow to the drips. You can do this a number of different ways, but the easiest method is to use one of Painter X's default effects.

**1.** In the Effects menu, select Objects > Create Drop Shadow. The options box appears (Figure 3.39).

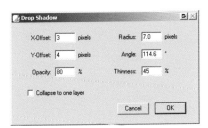

**Figure 3.39** The Drop Shadow options box

**2.** Change the default settings to the following:

- X-Offset: 3 pixels
- Y-Offset: 4 pixels
- Opacity: 80%
- Radius: 7.0 pixels
- Angle: 114.6°
- Thinness: 45%

**3.** Deselect the Collapse To One Layer box if it is marked, and click OK.

**4.** A new layer group is created that includes the original Drip layer and the drop shadow. Ungroup the Drip layer and the Shadow layer by clicking on the Layer Commands button at the bottom left of the Layers palette. Alternatively, you can use the keyboard commands Ctrl+U (⌘+U on the Mac).

**5.** Select the Drip layer and duplicate it.

**6.** The duplicate layer will be the active layer by default, but if it is not, click on the duplicate to select it.

**7.** From the Effects menu, select Surface Control > Apply Surface Texture. The options box appears where the sliders should be moved to the following settings:

- Using: Paper
- Softness: 8.4
- Amount: 28%
- Shine: 65%
- Leave the other settings at the default.

A paper texture with a large pattern works best. You can change the paper texture while the Apply Surface Texture options box is open. Select different paper textures, and watch their individual effect in the preview window (Figure 3.40).

**8.** Click the OK button. Figure 3.41 shows the image with the surface texture applied.

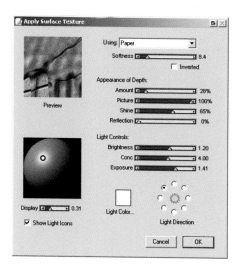

**Figure 3.40** The Apply Surface Texture options box showing a preview of the effect on the Drip layer

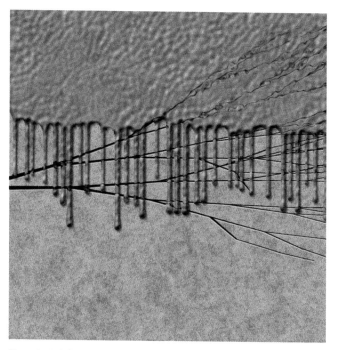

**Figure 3.41** A shiny surface texture is applied to the Drip layer.

Unfortunately, the application of the surface texture has affected the appearance of the drips in a negative way, making them not as clear. Using the Eraser brush with a large size, erase the drips portion of the top layer. The underlying Drip layer is revealed with the original drips visible. These drips are much clearer and more attractive (Figure 3.42).

Finally, add some highlights to each drip to finish the image.

9. Create a new layer. Choose the Glow brush from the FX brush category, and add the highlights. Figure 3.43 shows the finished image.

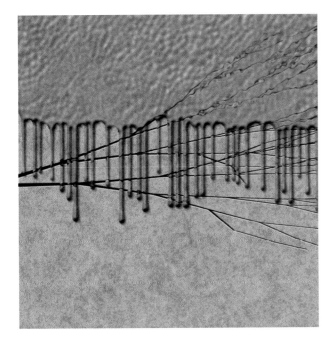

**Figure 3.42** The results of erasing the top layer of drips

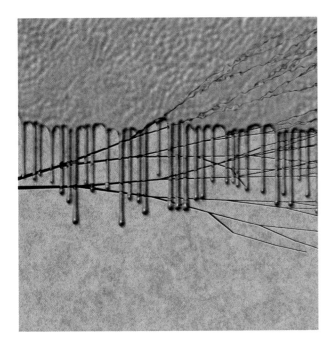

**Figure 3.43** Highlights are added to each drip.

## Final Thoughts

In this multipart tutorial, you learned a way to create a rocky texture, add a wet coating to the rocks, and make the wet surface appear thicker and gooey.

The techniques shown are just a small scratch on the surface of the multiple ways of accomplishing similar tasks. These techniques are but the starting point for your own experimentation.

# Painting a Fantasy Forest with the Image Hose

**4**

*The Image Hose may be one of the most overlooked features in Painter X, possibly because the default nozzles that ship with the program are based on photographs, so they are of limited use when you paint an image. Who, after all, wants photographic elements in the middle of their painted piece? The default nozzles tend to look inconsistent with most painting techniques and are generally ignored. But the Image Hose is a wonderful tool when used correctly; it can make painting small repeatable elements easy and quick. There is no better tool for painting multiples like leaves, pebbles, flowers, sand, and clouds.*

**Chapter Contents**

Using the Image Hose
Setting Up the Image
Painting Trees in the Forest
Adding Leaves to the Trees
Finishing Touches

## Using the Image Hose

The key to using the Image Hose correctly is to learn to build your own nozzles from art you paint. When you create your own nozzle materials, you guarantee that the style and look in your painting will be consistent. This chapter scratches the surface of building nozzles by creating a few simple ones to use in the painting.

The true depth and potential of creating your own nozzles is best learned by experimentation and therefore is really beyond the scope of this book. But using the simple techniques presented here, you can go on to expand your knowledge of how to best make nozzles that work for your particular style of painting.

## Setting Up the Image

There is really nothing special about setting up the image you are going to paint on, but it is sometimes good to go over the basics just to make sure that everything in the rest of the tutorial works correctly. For example, if a brush size is specified in the tutorial but the image being painted on is different from the one in the tutorial, you might experience unexpected difficulties.

So it is best to start at the beginning.

1. Create a new image at 1600×1200.

2. Launch the Gradient palette if it is not already visible, and choose the Two Point gradient.

3. Edit a gradient to produce a nice transition from a light sky blue to a light blue-green color (Figure 4.1).

**Figure 4.1** The Gradient Editor

4. Move the red button around the gradient preview so blue is at the top and turquoise is at the bottom.

5. Fill the Canvas layer to create a nicely gradiated sky, as you can see in Figure 4.2.

6. Create a new layer on which to paint a hill shape.

7. Using the Pen tool, draw a low, nicely curved hill shape.

8. Convert the shape you just created to a selection.

    The Shape layer disappears, and an active selection becomes visible. Right now the canvas is the active layer, so make sure that you click on the layer you just created to make it the active layer.

9. Fill the selection with a light greenish-gray color (Figure 4.3).

**Figure 4.2** The gradient is applied to the Canvas layer for the background sky.

**Figure 4.3** The shape is converted to a selection and then filled with an earthy color on a new layer.

Using the same technique, create two additional Hill layers above the first one. The color of each hill should get darker as it gets closer to the viewer. Each hill should be on its own layer (Figure 4.4).

**Figure 4.4** Two additional Hill layers are created.

Save the image. Now it is time to paint the trees.

## Painting Trees in the Forest

The tree trunks are not particularly hard to paint. They will be stylized and are not meant to mimic natural trees. If you do not want to paint stylized trees, go ahead and paint more natural and realistic tree trunks. Either stylized or realistic trees will work for later techniques. The secret is that the few trees that will be painted here will be used to paint larger numbers of trees later by creating a nozzle file you can use with the Image Hose.

### Painting a Few Trees to Produce a Forest

So, let's paint some trees.

1. Create a new layer and paint a tree trunk using the Captured Bristle variant in the Acrylics category and a darker greenish color. Rotate the canvas to make drawing the trunk easier if necessary. Do not paint form—no light or shadow on the trunk at this time.

2. Draw branches at almost right angles. Keep things simple as in Figure 4.5.

3. Using the same brush in various sizes, gradually add more branches and lighter colors until the trunk looks more three-dimensional. Don't worry about the ragged and rough edges. We'll clean up the edges of the trunk and branches later with the Eraser (Figure 4.6).

**Figure 4.6** More branches and some lighter colors are added to the tree trunk.

Draw a few more trees on different layers. A quick way to accomplish the task is to do the following:

**4.** Copy an existing tree.

**5.** Paste it into a new layer, flip the tree horizontally, erase some of the existing branches and paint on new ones, or cut existing branches, paste them into a new layer, transform them in different ways, and then combine the branches with the original layer.

While using the same tree as the basis for additional trees speeds the process, there is the danger that all the trees will look remarkably similar. Make sure that you paint some variation within each tree.

The number of trees that you create is completely a personal choice. Usually you will want at least four or five trees, or you will notice too much repeating of individual tree elements. For example, if you have a knothole in your original tree and create only a few variants, you will notice an unrealistic pattern created by the knothole repeating itself. In this instance, I have created seven trees, each on a different layer. Figure 4.7 shows all seven of the trees that I created from the single original tree.

**Figure 4.7** The first seven trees created for the fantasy forest

### Creating a Nozzle File of the Trees

Now that we have painted a number of different trees and placed them on different layers, we will combine them into a nozzle file that can be used with the Image Hose brush to paint a forest.

1.  Select each Tree layer by clicking on it in the Layers palette while holding the Shift key; choose the Layer Adjuster tool in the toolbox and, with the Auto Select Layer box checked, drag over the layers you want to select in the document window, or click on the small menu arrow at the top right of the Layers palette and choose Select All Layers.

2.  Group the selected layers using the Group Layers command in the Layers menu, or use the keyboard combination Ctrl+G (⌘+G on the Mac).

3.  With the Tree layer group selected, go to the nozzle icon to display the Nozzle palette. Click the small menu arrow to the upper right of the Nozzle palette and select Make Nozzle From Group.

A new image is immediately created from the trees in the grouped layer. Each tree is placed on a grid whose size is determined by the largest tree in the group of layers. The new image has a black background, as you can see in Figure 4.8.

**Figure 4.8** The new nozzle image created when the Make Nozzle From Group command is selected

Save the file in the native Painter RIF format; when naming the file, add the suffix nozzle to the image name. You should add this suffix so you can find the nozzle images easily among all your saved files. In this case, I named the new image tree nozzle.rif.

Return to the original image.

4. Hide the grouped Tree layer, but don't delete it. You'll use these trees later.

5. Pick the Brush tool and select the Tree Painter brush from the Book Brush library. Make the brush about 85 pixels in size.

6. Load the Tree Nozzle file. (This file is available for download.)

7. Create a new layer above the canvas, and paint a line of trees across the width of the background (Figure 4.9).

8. Name the layer Trees01 to avoid confusion with the multiple layers that you'll create.

9. Transform the layer slightly in the vertical dimension so the bottom of the trees is below the hill line. If needed, move the Tree layer down slightly using the Layer Adjuster tool.

10. Copy and paste the canvas into a layer above the Tree layer you just painted. You'll use this layer to adjust the value and colors of the trees behind them.

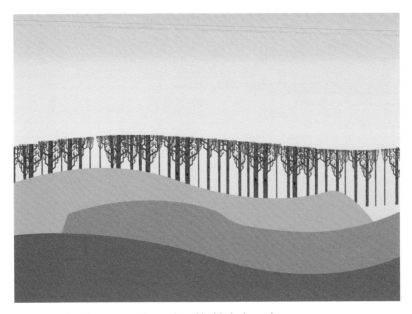

**Figure 4.9** A line of trees is painted across the width of the background.

For the remainder of this tutorial, each time the canvas is pasted above a Tree layer, we'll refer to it as the Tinting layer.

**11.** Lower the Opacity setting of this new Tinting layer to about 80%. The tree trunks now look much lighter and visually blend into the background (Figure 4.10).

It's possible to adjust the value and color of the background trees in several ways to accomplish the same effect, but I find that the method described allows a lot of flexibility should adjustments need to be made in the future.

**Figure 4.10** The Canvas layer is copied and pasted, and the Opacity setting is reduced to cover the tree line.

## A Second Row of Trees

Forests have depth, and we need to create additional rows of trees to give our image that illusion. To create the second row of trees

1. Create a new layer just above the first Tinting layer.

2. Pick the Brush tool, and once again select the Tree Painter brush. Make the brush size about 150 pixels.

3. Load the Tree Nozzle file.

4. Paint a second row of trees that follows the contour of the hill, and name the new layer Trees02 (Figure 4.11).

**Figure 4.11** A second row of trees is painted on a new layer following the contour of the hill.

5. Select the Free Transform tool.

6. The icon for the Trees02 layer in the palette changes to indicate that the layer has changed to a Reference layer. An eight-handled box surrounds the new trees. It has four corner handles and four side handles.

7. Drag the bottom side handle down to lengthen the trees and hide their bases behind the Hill layer (Figure 4.12).

8. Right-click on the Trees02 layer and commit the transform. The Reference layer is changed back to a default layer.

9. Paste another copy of the canvas as a Tinting layer above the Trees02 layer (Figure 4.13).

10. Select the Trees02 layer and load a selection from the Select menu. When the Options box opens, select Tree02 Transparency and click OK (Figure 4.14). A marquee surrounds the transparent areas of the Trees02 layer.

**Figure 4.12** The bases of the trees are hidden behind the hill using the Free Transform tool.

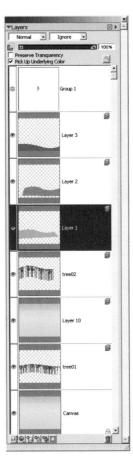

**Figure 4.13** Another copy of the Tinting layer is pasted over the Trees02 layer.

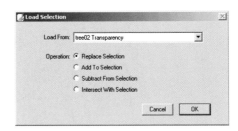

**Figure 4.14** The Load Selection dialog box with Trees02 Transparency selected

11. Invert the selection using the Select menu or use the key combination Ctrl+Shift+I (⌘+Shift+I on the Mac).

12. Click on the Tinting layer covering the Tree02 layer so it is active. The selection is still active and displaying the *marching ants* marquee.

13. Press the Backspace key. Most of the Tinting layer is deleted, leaving only those portions that cover the trees on the layer below.

14. Lower the Opacity setting of the active layer to about 60%. The trees are now about the same value and color as the hill they are on (Figure 4.15).

15. To reduce the number of layers, select both the Tree02 layer and the background layer above it and collapse the two using the Collapse command under the Layer Commands button at the bottom left of the Layers palette. You can also use the Collapse command in the Layers menu or the Crtl+Shift+X keys (⌘+Shift+X on the Mac).

**Figure 4.15** The second layer of trees now appear to be about the same color and value as the hill they are on.

## A Third Row of Trees

We'll go on to create the third row of trees in our painting. Each layer is created in essentially the same manner, with only slight variations.

1. Create a new layer behind the second hill and name it Trees03.

2. Size the Tree Painter brush to 200 pixels.

3. Load the Tree Nozzle file, and paint a third row of trees following the contour of the second hill (Figure 4.16).

4. Using the Free Transform tool, drag the bottom side handle down and lengthen the tree trunks to again hide their bases behind the Hill layer.

**Figure 4.16** The third row of trees is painted using a larger brush and following the contour of the second hill shape.

**5.** With the top side handle, scale the tops of the trees into the top quarter of the image (Figure 4.17).

**6.** Right-click the image and commit to a default layer.

**7.** Paste a new Tinting layer over the Trees03 layer.

**8.** Load a selection using the Trees03 transparency.

**9.** Invert the selection.

**Figure 4.17** The tops and bottoms of the trees have been scaled using the Free Transform tool.

10. Select the Tinting layer and use the Backspace key to clear the layer except for the areas that cover the trees.

11. Lower the Opacity setting of the layer to around 34% (Figure 4.18).

12. You can determine the exact Opacity setting while looking at your own painting. Collapse the Trees03 and Tinting layers together.

**Figure 4.18** The colors are adjusted on the third layer of trees.

## A Fourth Row of Trees

The remaining row of trees is painted using the same method. The only parts of the sequence that are different are the size of the brush used and the opacity of the background.

1. Create a new layer behind the Front Hill layer.

2. Using the Tree Painter brush and the Tree Nozzle sized to about 285 pixels, paint a row of trees running parallel to the Front Hill layer. Name the layer Trees04.

3. Use the Free Transform tool to scale the trees so the bottoms are below and behind the Front Hill layer and the treetops reach the top of the picture.

4. Commit the transform.

5. Paste another Tinting layer above Trees04.

6. Load a selection based on the transparency of the Trees04 layer.

7. Invert the selection.

8. Select the tinting layer and use the Backspace key to delete the tint except that portion that covers Trees04.

9. Lower the Opacity setting of the Tinting layer to about 10%.

10. Collapse Trees04 and its Tinting layer.

There are now four rows of trees made from the original painted tree. Each row appears to fade into the distant background. The image should look something like Figure 4.19.

**Figure 4.19** The four rows of trees are painted from one original tree.

### Foreground Trees

The final step for our forest is to add the foreground trees. We will not paint these trees with the Image Hose. Instead, we will use the trees we painted originally.

1.  Select the top layer group. This layer group is hidden from view, but it should hold all the original trees, with each on its own layer.

2.  Unhide the layer by clicking on the eye icon to the left side of the layer group.

3.  Ungroup this layer group using the keys Ctrl+U (⌘+U on the Mac), or in the Layers menu select Ungroup.

4.  Pick a few of the individual trees, and arrange their layers nicely in the foreground of the image using the Layers Adjuster. You will probably not want to use all the trees (Figure 4.20). You can delete those trees that you don't use.

    The foreground trees may look very close in value and color to the second row of trees. To make these trees advance into the foreground and separate from the second row of trees, we need to darken their value and alter their color.

5.  Select each front tree. In the Effects menu, choose Tonal Control > Adjust Colors. Darken the trees using the Value slider.

6.  Warm the color of each tree using the Hue Shift slider.

7.  Increase the color strength of the trees using the Saturation slider.

**Figure 4.20** Individual Tree layers are arranged to make the closest part of the forest.

The level of change is up to you. I lowered the value about 30%, increased the Saturation about 11%, and moved the Hue Shift slider –15%.

The front few trees are now distinctly darker and warmer than those behind them (Figure 4.21).

**Figure 4.21** The colors in the front line of trees are adjusted to be darker and warmer.

## Adding Leaves to the Trees

In this section, we will add leaves to all the different Tree layers using a custom-made nozzle. The beauty of this technique is that we can paint large numbers of repetitive shapes with little effort.

Unlike the Tree nozzle used to paint the trunks of the trees, where we painted each tree trunk at the same size and in the same orientation, the Leaves nozzle rotates the individual elements and randomly places them on the canvas to give a natural feeling to the groups of leaves.

Just like with the Trees nozzle created earlier, the Leaves nozzle will need a number of individual painted leaves and some groups of leaves. Each leaf or group of leaves painted for the nozzle must be on an individual layer.

### Creating a Leaf Brush

It is easiest to paint the leaves that will make up the nozzle file by creating a new leaf-shaped brush based on a leaf-shaped dab. Actual leaf brushes we create are the most useful in many cases.

When we create a new brush, it takes its attributes from the currently active brush. Therefore, we need to consider which brush to use as the base. If the Eraser brush is active, the newly created brush would also be an eraser, which is probably not what we want. While we can make enough changes to an eraser so that it eventually paints instead of erases, it is easier to just start with a brush that is close to the intended look of the final brush.

1. As a base brush, select the Flat Color variant from the Pens category in the Brush Selector.

2. Draw a leaf shape in a new image. The background should be white and the leaf should be black. While the size of the image is not critical, the drawn leaf should not be much larger than 100 pixels on a side.

3. Drag a roughly square selection around the leaf shape using the Rectangular Selection tool in the toolbox.

4. Click the menu arrow in the upper-right corner of the Brush Selector and choose Capture Dab.

The leaf dab is now captured and loaded as the dab in the base brush. We need to adjust the brush settings before the new leaf brush variant will actually draw leaves. We can make all the needed adjustments to the new brush in the Brush Creator.

5. Open the Brush Creator using the keyboard combination Ctrl+B (⌘+B) or the Show Brush Creator found in the Window menu.

6. In the Brush Creator, make sure that the Stroke Designer is active. The Stroke Designer is the right tab at the top left of the preview window (Figure 4.22).

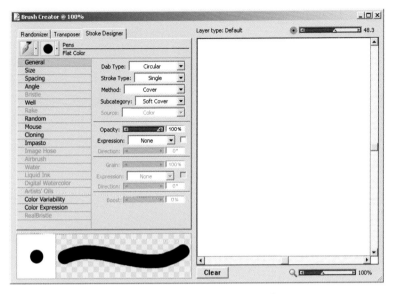

**Figure 4.22** The Brush Creator window showing the Stroke Designer tab.

**7.** Enter the following values in the Stroke Designer. If an option isn't mentioned, don't change its setting.

- General Category **Cover**
  Subcategory **Soft Cover**
  Opacity **100%**
  Expression **None**
- Size Min Size **60%**
  Expression **Random**
- Spacing Spacing **150%**
  Min Spacing **10**
- Angle Squeeze **99%**
  Expression **Random**
  Ang Range **360°**
- Random Jitter **4.0**
  Expression **Random**

**8.** Close the Brush Creator by using the keyboard combination Ctrl+B or by clicking the X in the upper-right corner.

**9.** In the Brush Selector, click the menu arrow and choose Save Variant. Name the brush Leaf and click OK. A new brush variant of the Pens category named Leaf is created. To select the new brush, just select its icon. The icon for the brush is usually created at the bottom of the variant list.

**10.** Go back into the menu on the Brush Selector and click Restore Variant to take the original Flat Color brush back to its default setting.

The Leaf brush will now paint a pretty good row of leaves. It would be tedious, though, to try to paint a large number of leaves using this brush since it only paints single leaf dabs. Creating a Leaf nozzle based on this Leaf brush will allow us to paint large numbers of leaves very quickly using the Image Hose.

### Creating a Leaf Nozzle

The steps used to create the new Leaf nozzle are the same as those used to create the Tree Trunk nozzle earlier in the chapter. If you need detailed instructions, please refer to that section.

To create a Leaf nozzle based on the Leaf brush, follow these steps:

1. Create a new image. Something about 400×400 pixels is large enough.

2. In the new image, create about 10 new layers. The actual number is not critical as long as there are enough layers to produce a random-looking brush stroke.

3. Starting on the top layer, paint some leaves using the new leaves brush. The color of the leaves does not really matter for this particular nozzle, but since these are leaves, green is as good a color as any other.

4. Hide the layer and move down to the next.

Hiding each layer is only a matter of convenience and helps us keep track of which layer we are painting on and what we are painting on it. The more layers we use in a nozzle, the more helpful it will be to hide each layer as we finish painting on it.

The layers shouldn't have too many leaves. Some layers may have only one or two leaves.

5. Continue painting, hiding, and moving down to the next layer until all 10 layers have leaves on them. Don't paint leaves on the background.

6. Unhide all the layers.

7. Select and group all the layers. The instructions are the same as described earlier when making the Tree nozzle.

8. From the Nozzle palette, select Make Nozzle From Group.

9. Save the file as `Leaves nozzle` in the native Painter RIF format.

Now that we've created the Leaf brush and a new Leaves nozzle, it is time to add some foliage to the trees.

### Adding Foliage to the Trees

Hiding all Tree layers except for the one we are using makes it easier to see how thickly we are painting the leaves. As we finish each layer of leaves, we'll unhide the next Tree Trunk layer.

1. Hide all the Tree Trunk layers except the farthest one.

2. Start with the farthest line of trees and create a new layer above the background layer that is on top of the tree trunks.

3. Activate the secondary color on the Colors palette by clicking on the secondary color. A thicker outline indicates that the secondary color is selected.

4. Use the color picker and select a color from the trunks of the farthest trees. The secondary color updates to reflect the color selected.

5. Pick the Leaf Painter variant of the Image Hose brush category. The brush is available in the Book Brushes category.

**Note:** This variant is available in the downloadable set of brushes associated with this book.

6. Set the Grain amount in the Brush Options bar at the top of the working space to 0%. This setting causes the Image Hose to paint with the secondary color without regard to the original colors in the Image Hose.

7. Set the size of the brush so the leaves are painted an appropriate size compared to the tree trunks.

8. Paint bunches of leaves on the tops of the distant trees. Make sure to do this on the new layer in case you need to make changes.

The number of leaves you paint is completely up to you. The image will now look something like Figure 4.23.

9. Unhide the next layer of tree trunks, and create a new layer above them.

10. Resize the Leaf Painter brush so the leaves are painted a bit larger than the far background ones.

**Figure 4.23** The farthest leaves are painted on the tops of the tree trunks in the distant background.

11. As the tree trunks get closer, you will see some variation between the light and dark colors in the trunks. Set the secondary color to the darker of the colors in the tree using the color picker, and paint leaves in the new layer on top of the second row of tree trunks.

12. Select the lighter color in the tree trunks, and paint some lighter leaves on top of the darker ones. You may want to make several additional selections from the tree trunks and paint more leaves with those colors.

13. Use the same technique with the third and fourth rows of trees (Figure 4.24).

**Figure 4.24** Leaves are painted on each row of trees.

Now we'll finish the last two rows of trees. The painting now has a sense of depth and is quite detailed. And we've done all this using only a few initial images.

14. Unhide the foreground tree trunks.

15. Create a new layer for the leaves.

16. Pick the colors for the leaves from the tree trunks, and paint the forest canopy (Figure 4.25).

17. When you've finished painting all the leaves, click the foreground color to make it active.

**Figure 4.25** The foreground canopy of the forest is painted in using colors selected from the tree trunks.

### Painting Undergrowth and Shrubs on the Hills

The trees themselves are looking good, but the hills are looking a bit sparse. We need to add some undergrowth to each of the Hill layers as they recede into the distance. Fortunately, painting the undergrowth is no more difficult than painting the trees and leaves.

Once again, work from the background of the painting toward the foreground as when you painted the leaves. Hide the Tree layers, and reveal them as you work forward. You do not need to hide the Hill layers, though, as the ground cover is painted.

1. Create a new layer above the Background Hill layer.

2. Select the color of the Background Hill layer. Then select the Brush tool and pick the Graphic Paintbrush Soft variant from the F-X brush category and paint some rough bushy shapes on the new layer over the Far Hill layer (Figure 4.26).

   Now we'll move on to the next hill.

3. Create a new layer above the second hill.

4. Use the Grass Painter brush with one of the grass paper textures to paint grassy shapes on the new layer above the second hill.

5. Switch to Dons GFX Paint brush and, using a pattern that is similar to the paper texture in the previous step, paint a series of grassy shapes along the top of the second hill.

**Figure 4.26** The distant hill is covered with undergrowth using the Graphic Paintbrush Soft variant.

Two of the hills are complete, with one hill left. The painting is looking more and more like a fantasy forest.

6. Continue painting the undergrowth on the foreground hill using the same technique used for the second hill. In the front hill, vary the color more than in the further ones (Figure 4.27). As objects move closer to the viewer in the landscape, their colors are clearer and easier to distinguish.

**Figure 4.27** The undergrowth in the foreground is painted using more variety in the color.

Our final touch to the forest undergrowth is to add a few shrubs.

**7.** Create one more new layer on top of all the other layers.

**8.** Use the Leaf Painter Image Hose brush and the Leaves nozzle to paint some shrubbery in the front of the scene (Figure 4.28).

The colors of the closest leaves should be brighter than any of the other leaves in the image.

**Figure 4.28** Shrubbery has been added to the front of the forest.

For all intents and purposes, we could consider the painting of the forest as finished now, but adding a few additional creative touches can take a rather ordinary finished painting and elevate it to a new level. The next section covers a few finishing touches that we can add to the forest to make the image more interesting.

## Finishing Touches

We have painted all the scene's elements. The whole painting has a graphic feel that is consistent with the feel of the painting. All that is left is to add a few finishing touches.

Now we will add some shadows on the front and second rows of tree trunks, a few streaks of light filtering through the forest canopy, some dust motes in the atmosphere, and maybe a bird or two.

### Enhancing the Scene with Shadows

Adding some shadows on the tree trunks is easy, and the shadows will dramatically enhance the appearance of the scene. We'll add shadows for both the first and second rows of tree trunks on their own layer. The Trees layers that are deeper in the background will not benefit from adding shadows.

To add shadows to the first row of tree trunks

1. Create a new layer on top of the first row of tree trunks.

2. Change the Composite Method of the new layer to either Gel or Multiply. Either works equally well.

3. Load a selection based on the transparency of the first layer of tree trunks.

4. With the selection still active, move back to the new Multiply layer.

5. Use the Leaf Painter brush, a mid-value gray as the secondary color, and the Grain amount set to 0 in the Brush Options menu at the top of the screen. Then paint some shadows on the tree trunks (Figure 4.29).

Because a selection is loaded based on the Tree Trunk layer's transparency, the shadows are painted only on the trunks and not into any of the background.

**Figure 4.29** Shadows are added to the tree trunks..

If the selection marquee is distracting, it's possible to hide it in the Select menu by choosing Hide Marquee.

6. After you paint the leaves, select the Digital airbrush or another airbrush of your choice. Paint the shadow sides of the tree trunks on the same layer as the leaves shadows using the same gray color (Figure 4.30).

7. Deselect the layer using either the Select menu or the keyboard combination Ctrl+D (⌘+D on the Mac). This is particularly important if you hid the marquee in an earlier step.

Sometimes if the marquee is hidden, it is easy to forget that there is a still a selection. More than one artist has become extremely frustrated trying to paint in an image and not being able to make a mark because a hidden selection is active.

**Figure 4.30** Using an airbrush, shadows are added to the trunks of the trees on the same layer as the leaves' shadows.

We'll add shadows to the second row of trees using the same technique as before.

1. Create a new layer above the second row of trees and set it to either Multiply or Gel.

2. Load a selection from the second row of trees transparency.

3. Add shadows on the trunks using the same brushes used earlier (Figure 4.31).

**Figure 4.31** Shadows are added to the trunks of the second row of trees.

4. Slightly blur each Shadow layer using Effects > Focus > Soften. The default setting of 3.0 is fine.
5. To finish the shadows, collapse each Shadow layer with its respective Tree Trunk layer.

## Adding Light

The next finishing touch is to add some streaks of light filtering through the forest canopy. The process is not difficult and produces some attractive results.

1. Use the Pen tool to draw some shapes that will be used as the basis for the rays of light (Figure 4.32).

Figure 4.32 The Pen tool is used to draw some shapes that will be used to create streaks of light shining through the forest canopy.

2. Convert the shapes to selections using Convert to Selection in the Shapes menu.
3. Feather the selection 15 pixels.
4. Save the selection just in case you make a mistake. It is much quicker to load a saved selection than it is to redraw shapes.
5. Create a new layer above the second row of trees.
6. If the selection created earlier is not active, load the selection just saved.
7. Using the Pixel Spray variant from the Airbrush category and a light yellow-green color, paint in the streaks starting in the top left and gradually fading to no color about three-quarters down the selection.
8. Deselect the layer and use the Soften effect in the Effects > Focus menu; soften the layer with a setting of about 10.
9. Lower the Opacity setting of thc layer to 50%.

   There are now some rays of light shining through the trees (Figure 4.33).

**Figure 4.33** Rays of light have been created above the second layer of trees.

## Adding Dust Motes

When you see streaks of light up close, there are usually small dust particles randomly floating through them. We will add a few motes of dust to our light streaks.

1. Create a new layer above the Light Streaks layer.

2. Use the Tiny Spattery Airbrush variant found in the Airbrush category to add some dust motes in the atmosphere. Use a light touch, and do not overdo the effect.

3. Soften the Dust Mote layer using a setting of 2.

4. Lower the Opacity setting of the Dust Mote layer to about 50%. Now the dust motes add a subtle shimmer to the atmosphere, as in Figure 4.34.

**Figure 4.34** Dust motes have been added to a new layer using the Tiny Spattery Airbrush.

## Adding a Little More Light and Dust

We will add another set of light rays in the foreground.

1. Create a new layer on top of all other layers.

2. Load the saved light rays selection.

3. Use the Digital airbrush and paint streaks of light on the new layer.

4. Deselect the layer and soften using a value of 10.

5. Lower the Opacity setting of the layer to between 30 and 50%.

These streaks should not duplicate the ones on the lower layer even though they were created using the same selection.

6. To change the size and shape of the new streaks, use Free Transform. Scale the streaks so they are larger, and rotate them so their angle is similar to the lower streaks.

7. When the light streaks are positioned as you want them, change the Reference Layer back to a default layer by right-clicking the layer and picking Commit.

8. Create a new layer and add more dust motes as in the earlier steps (Figure 4.35).

Figure 4.35   Dust motes are added on top of the Light Rays layer.

## Adding Fauna in the Flora

The image is just about finished. For a nice final touch, we'll add just a little bit of animal life to the painting. In this case, a small red bird would complement the color scheme nicely.

We won't use any tricks with layers, special brushes, or image effects to add the bird. We'll simply create a new layer and paint the animal (Figure 4.36).

**Figure 4.36** A small red bird is painted on a new layer to add a bit of life to the forest scene.

## Putting a Soft Focus on Reality

Our last step is to add a subtle lighting effect to the whole painting.

Because the lighting effect won't work across layers, we need to clone the image. We can then apply the lighting effect to the clone and not the original painting.

1. Clone the image using the File menu and selecting the Clone command.

2. From the Effects menu, select Surface Control > Apply Lighting. The Apply Lighting options box opens (Figure 4.37).

3. Select the third lighting scheme, called Splashy Color.

4. Click OK to apply the effect (Figure 4.38).

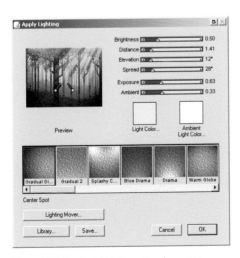

**Figure 4.37** The Apply Lighting options box opens.

**Figure 4.38** The Apply Lighting effect is applied to the image.

Sometimes the effect is too strong, and in this image it has darkened the bottom of the painting too much. An easy way to adjust the amount of the effect is to select the Fade command from the Edit menu.

The Fade command reduces the applied effect to any percentage specified by moving the slider.

5. Select Fade from the Edit menu. Then set the Fade slider to 50% and click OK (Figure 4.39).

The painting is finished!

**Figure 4.39** The lighting effect is reduced in strength by 50% using the Fade command.

## Final Thoughts

Knowing how to use the Image Hose is invaluable. And knowing how to create custom nozzles to fit perfectly any project at hand will make your work stand out from the crowd. It is not unusual for others to ask how you painted a particular effect or comment on how long it must have taken to create a particular passage in a painting. As the artist, you can just smile at such comments and keep your secret to yourself.

This chapter covered the Image Hose and looked at creating a custom brush. If you take the time to learn how to create custom brushes, your work will benefit.

The intelligent use of layers will always benefit the digital artist, and while there was nothing particularly unusual about their use in this chapter's image, it is a good example of how to use layers to build depth into a painting.

The main idea to take away from this painting tutorial is the power and flexibility of the Image Hose. It may be one of Painter's least-appreciated yet most powerful tools.

# Painting the Sleepwalker

*This tutorial features a sleepwalker walking down the middle of a hall in the dead of night. He is carrying a candle to light the way on his nightly travels.*

*You may be wondering why this particular subject matter has been chosen for a tutorial. The explanation is simple. This digital painting contains a number of different objects and effects that often cause painters difficulty.*

**Chapter Contents**

# Painting a Night Scene

In this chapter, I demonstrate a way to paint several different objects that often present problems for painters. Several of these problems are specific to darkly lit or night scenes. The objects that will be painted include a candle, a dark scene with minimal color differences, a patterned surface, moonlight through a window, and smoke.

It is not important to duplicate the physical properties of the candlelight, the light shining through the window, or the smoke accurately. What is important is that the process results in a believable piece of art.

There are probably as many different ways to paint these subjects as there are artists. I don't claim that my way is the best way, but the method that I use is one that works and gives satisfactory results.

I will present a few techniques that quickly achieve specific looks or effects. These techniques include the following approaches:

- Arranging layers to achieve specific effects
- Using the Auto Paint feature to save time and paint a surface with greater regularity than can be done by hand
- Using cloning
- Using some of the Distortion brushes to help quickly paint smoke
- Using Lighting Effects
- Applying a surface texture as the finishing touch

Some of this tutorial relies on your ability to draw and paint. After you use all the tricks and techniques, the ultimate success of the image will depend on your skills as an artist. If you are a beginning artist, have patience and do your best. If you are more advanced in your artistic skills, experiment rather than just following along. Whatever your skill level, have fun, and use the lessons you learn in your own work.

As the tutorials progress in this book, I will devote less and less space to explaining where a specific command, tool, or feature is located. It is assumed that you have a working knowledge of Painter X, and we will spend the majority of the time in the actual technique and not locating program features, commands, or tools.

## Setting Up the Image

This tutorial is based on a doodle from one of my sketch books (Figure 5.1). You are encouraged to start with your own drawing. If you would rather follow each step a little more closely, the original sketch is available for you to download and use.

The brushes and paper textures used in this tutorial are also available to download if you have not done so earlier.

There's no reason why you can't just open the sketch and start painting directly on top of the drawing. Often that is exactly the approach I will use. In the long run, though, taking a few minutes to set up the sketch will save time later in the painting process and often make for a less frustrating experience.

**Figure 5.1** The original scan of the sleepwalker sketch

Setting up the image is not difficult. A few small adjustments to the sketch, and we'll be ready to go.

1. Open the sleepwalker sketch.

2. Select the entire sketch; cut and paste it back into the image.

3. Duplicate the Sketch layer, or paste another version into the image.

4. Change the Composite Method of the top Sketch layer to Multiply or Gel. All the white and near white in the sketch become transparent.

5. Hide and lock the top layer. You might use the hidden Sketch layer to reference the original sketch if needed later in the painting.

When we've finished the painting, we'll no longer need this hidden Sketch layer and can delete it.

### Tinting the Sketch to a Different Color

The original sketch is visible as black lines on a white background. Often when I begin a painting from a sketch, I want the drawing to be tinted using colors that will be used in the painting. There are several methods of tinting the line work in a drawing. Which method we use depends on how we'll use the line work in the painting.

In this case, we want to tint the sketch to make the drawing harmonious with the colors that we will use in the painting. We will eventually cover most of the drawing as the painting progresses, but there will no doubt be a few areas where bits and pieces of the sketch will show through. If the lines in the sketch are black, those areas may not be in harmony with the rest of the painting.

1. Create a new layer above the Sketch layer.

2. Fill the layer with a mid-value blue-gray color.

3. Change the Composite Method of the layer to Colorize.

Depending on how light or dark the color was that we used to fill the layer, the sketch now takes on that color. It's best to avoid very saturated colors because they tend to burn out the lighter areas of the sketch. Also, at a certain point, lightening the color no longer changes the appearance of the sketch. Generally, the best results are with colors that are not too light or dark and not too saturated.

4. Collapse the Blue layer with the Sketch layer. Name the layer blue sketch.

The sketch is a nice bluish color that will go well with the colors that we will use in the painting. Any parts of the sketch that show through the painted colors will not disrupt the color harmony of the painting (Figure 5.2).

**Figure 5.2** The black colors of the sketch are tinted a dark blue color.

Colorizing a drawing this way is a great way to get rid of a black sketch.

We will use the tinted sketch as a guide to paint the sleepwalker. One thing to avoid when using a sketch as a guide is that you do not get into a coloring book mode. We were all complimented as children when we showed our parents the crayon colorings we did as we were developing some motor control. The praises we received were great if we "stayed in the lines" of the images in the coloring book.

The lines of this sketch are only a guide, and you will not receive praise if you carefully try to stay inside the borders defined by them.

## Setting the Value and Color of the Background

When beginning a painting, it is always a good idea to set the value and predominant color of the image as early as possible. This painting will be a night scene, so the color scheme will lean toward darker values. Blue is the predominant color, and orange is the accent color because the candle will be mainly oranges. The overall color harmony scheme will be complementary.

The first step is to change the Sketch layer to either Gel or Multiply. We want all the white to once again become transparent. Lower the Opacity setting of this Blue Sketch layer to 50%.

1. Create a new layer above the canvas but below the sketch.
2. Create a Two-Point gradient with a dark blue as the main color and dark violet as the additional color.
3. Pick Circular Gradient for the Gradient Type option. In the Gradient palette, the preview should show the violet in the center of the gradient, with a smooth transition to blue on the outside.
4. Using the Paint Bucket tool, fill the layer. Center the fill on the candle so the violet colors are concentrated there.

The color of what will become the wall in the painting is set (Figure 5.3). Now we need a floor for the sleepwalker.

**Figure 5.3** The colors of the wall are established.

**5.** Make a rectangular selection along the bottom of the Colored layer. The top of the selection should end at about ankle height on the character.

**6.** Fill the selection with the dark blue used in the gradient. This filled rectangle will become the floor (Figure 5.4).

When we build a digital painting, we should save selections for the basic areas within the image. The wall and floor are good examples. Saving selections for these areas will make it much easier to come back to them later in the painting. We may need to do additional work or make corrections, and being able to load a selection will allow us to do so without disturbing the surrounding parts of the painting. Selections are so easy to create at this stage that there is no excuse for not taking a moment to do so.

**Figure 5.4** The floor is filled with a dark blue.

### Creating Quick Selections for the Wall and Background

To create quick selections for the wall and floor do the following;

**1.** Pick the Magic Wand tool from the toolbox. Set the Tolerance to either 1 or 0. Tolerance levels limit the difference between the selected color and surrounding colors that are also selected. A low Tolerance level limits the selection to a narrow range of colors.

**2.** Click the Magic Wand tool in the floor color, and save the selection as Floor.

**3.** Invert the selection and save it as Wall.

That's about all there is setting up the image. We've set the basic colors of the painting, indicated the wall and floor planes, and have the beginnings of a light effect on the wall.

## Painting the Sleepwalker

We will start the image by putting a wallpaper pattern behind the character. Once again, there are several different ways to apply a repeating texture to a large flat area.

### Putting Up Wallpaper

To create the wallpaper, I will use the Auto Paint feature found in the Brush Selector menu. Auto Paint is a good feature to use when painting large flat areas because the strokes are painted in a much more consistent manner than we can do by hand.

1.   Create a layer above the wall. Check the Pick Up Underlying Color box if it is not already selected. Name the layer `Wallpaper`.

2.   Pick the Variable Chalk brush, and set the Grain to 10% in the Options bar.

3.   Load the Wall selection so only the wall is painted. You should see the marquee active around the entire wall.

4.   Open the Wallpaper paper library. You are given the option to append the currently loaded papers or load the Wallpaper library. Be careful with your choice. Loading the library overwrites all the textures in the Papers palette. If the textures are appended to the active paper library, all the textures in the new library are added to the current palette. You can also use the Paper Mover if you want to move just one or two of the wallpaper textures into your current library.

**Note:**  The library of wallpaper textures is available for download as a ZIP file at www.sybex .com/go/painter. If you have not already had the chance to download the papers, please do so. They are cross platform compatible and work on both PC and Mac.

5.   Choose one of the wallpaper textures. It is not important which one you choose.

6.   Pick the darkest blue in the background.

7.   Click the Brush Selector menu arrow and choose Record Stroke.

8.   Make a short stroke with the Variable Chalk brush on the new layer.

9.   Go back to the Brush Selector menu and choose Auto Playback.

Immediately, the brushstroke that was recorded paints the wallpaper texture into the new layer in a continuous series of randomly placed strokes. The computer speed, the size of the recorded stroke, and the size of the area being painted determine how long it takes to eventually fill the image with the stroke.

The beauty of Auto Playback is that it fills the area much quicker and with a more regular look than what we could do by hand.

10.   Let the playback continue until the whole background is covered.

11.   When the area is filled with strokes, just tap the cursor in the image to stop the Auto Playback.

**12.** As a final touch, lower the Opacity setting of the layer to 50% to make the wallpaper pattern subtle.

The wall is now filled with a repeating texture that should look like a wallpaper pattern. The pattern will be most visible over the lighter violet area and gradually fade into the darker blue edges (Figure 5.5).

To add some interest and a sense of realism to the painting, we need to add a glow to the wall where eventually we will paint the candle that the sleepwalker is carrying.

Painting a candle glow with traditional media can be a daunting process. It can be difficult to get a nice even transition of both color and value. Fortunately, this is easy to do with digital paint.

**Figure 5.5** The wall is covered with a pattern that looks like wallpaper.

We will paint two separate Glow layers. The first Glow layer is created to give a nice even transition from light around the candle to the violets in the background where the candlelight no longer has much influence.

**1.** Create a layer above the Wallpaper layer and name it Glow.

**2.** Draw a circular selection or drag the circular selection from the Selection Portfolio.

**3.** Resize and position the selection using the Selection Adjuster from the toolbox so its center is approximately over the candle flame.

**4.** Feather the selection 50 pixels. 50 is the maximum feather available in Painter.

**5.** Feather the selection again at the maximum 50 pixels.

**6.** Save the feathered selection in case it needs to be used later.

**7.** Fill the selection with a bright yellow/orange color.

8. Change the Composite Method of the layer to Colorize or Overlay. Colorize is my choice for the task.

9. Lower the layer's Opacity setting to 20%.

10. Soften the layer using the Soften effect found in the Effects > Focus menu. Set the Amount slider to the maximum value.

11. Soften the layer again using the same settings.

The first of two Glow layers is finished and positioned over the candle (Figure 5.6).

The second Glow layer is used to give more intensity right around the candle flame. It is created in a similar fashion to the first.

1. Duplicate the first Glow layer.

2. Change the Composite Method of the duplicate back to Default and fill with bright yellow. The Default Composite Method is used when filling the layer to help see the color of the fill accurately.

**Figure 5.6** The first Glow layer is positioned over the candle sketch.

3. Scale the layer to 50% of the original size. The exact size is not really important, but 50% is a good starting point.

4. Soften the layer.

5. Change the Composite Method to Colorize.

6. Set the Opacity to 30%.

7. Finally, position the Yellow layer over the candle flame using the Layer Adjuster tool (Figure 5.7).

**Figure 5.7** The small Glow layer is positioned over the spot where the candle flame will be painted.

If the smaller Glow layer is below the larger layer, we can reverse their positions so the smaller layer is on top.

In addition to painting the effects of light in the two Glow layers, we need to add some darks to give the painting more depth and atmosphere. We will use a lighting effect to darken the edges farthest away from the candle flame.

## Darkening the Image

The Apply Lighting effect is found under Effects > Surface Control menu. One would think that with the name Apply Lighting, the effect could be used only to lighten a painting, but I actually use it more often to darken a painting. I also use it to add an even gradient of color to layer in a painting.

One problem with the Apply Lighting effect is that we cannot apply it to a transparent layer. This makes it difficult to use in a multi-layered painting. Nonetheless, the effect is a valuable tool, and a work-around for the transparency issue is worth the effort.

Using Apply Lighting effectively in a multi-layer painting requires deciding exactly what parts of the painting need the effect. In this painting, we will apply the effect to the background. We will use only those layers that are part of the background.

1.  Select the Background layer.
2.  Duplicate the layer.
3.  Select the layer with the wallpaper painted on it.
4.  Duplicate the layer.

5. Shift-click the Duplicate Background and Duplicate Wallpaper layers. Both layers are selected.

6. Collapse the two selected layers into one.

7. With the new background layer active, choose Surface Control > Apply Lighting from the Effects menu.

8. In the options box that opens, choose the Warm Globe lighting scheme.

9. Move the light indicator so the smaller of the two circles is positioned at about ten o'clock, with the larger circle at about four o'clock.

10. Click OK.

The edges of the background are darkened, adding to the illusion that the candle is lighting the scene (Figure 5.8).

**Figure 5.8** The edges of the Background layer are darkened using the Apply Lighting effect.

We could delete the two original layers, but it is usually a good idea to keep them around just in case we need them somewhere down the line, so hide it and lock it, and the walls are finished for the moment.

We need to add a shadow under the sleepwalker character. We can do this in a number of different ways, but one of the easiest is to use an oval selection.

1. Create a new layer.

2. Pick the Circular Selection tool, and drag a long and thin oval selection on the new layer below the sleepwalker.

3. Use the Selection Adjuster tool to position the selection under the sleepwalking character.

4. Fill the selection with very dark blue.

5. Deselect the layer.

6. Blur the shadow using the Soften effect in the Effects > Focus menu. Set the amount of Soften to about 20.

7. Use the Layer Adjuster to fine-tune the placement of the shadow.

Of course, we can paint a more realistic shadow, but this simple one is perfectly adequate for the style of the painting (Figure 5.9).

**Figure 5.9** A shadow has been added to the floor, on a new layer, beneath the sleepwalker.

## Painting the Sleepwalking Character

We're finished with all the preliminary background work, so it's time to paint the sleepwalking character. To make painting just a bit easier, let's temporarily hide the Candle Glow layer. Hiding the Glow layer makes it easier to see the colors and values we are painting with when we work on the candle, the candleholder, and the hand.

1. Create a new layer under the visible Sketch layer.

2. Make sure that Pick Up Underlying Color is checked.

3. Name the layer Sleepwalker.

The layer we just created will be the one we paint the colors and values of the character on. We will do almost all the painting using the Variable Chalk variant found in the Chalk brush category. We will use a paper texture called Basic Paper from the Painter X default textures.

If you are feeling particularly creative, you can use any brush that has Cover as its method and the word Grainy in its Subcategory. If you have a favorite brush, by all means use it.

4. Quickly block in the basic colors on the character and candle. Do not worry about the small details until after all the main colors and shapes are painted.

5. Work from darker colors to lighter ones. This helps you get all the values in the darks painted correctly before you move on to the mid-tones and eventually to the lighter values. If you bounce around painting lights, mid-values, and darks, there is a greater chance that the painting will lack harmony.

We've painted the first colors. We don't need to make an effort to paint details. The main goal is simply to establish the color scheme. We've turned off the Glow layers to make it easier to see and paint the colors of the candle, candleholder, and hand (Figure 5.10).

**Figure 5.10** The first color is painted into the sleepwalker.

To continue painting the character, we need to combine the Sketch layer and first layer of color. Unfortunately, we cannot successfully collapse the Sketch layer and Basic Color layer into one layer. Because the Sketch layer has its Composite Method set to Multiply, all the white is displayed as transparent. If we collapse a Multiply layer with a Default layer that is partially transparent, the Multiply layer converts back to a Default layer, and all that apparent transparency changes back to solid white.

There is no convenient way to collapse only the Sketch and Color layers. We need to either collapse enough layers so that there is nothing displayed as transparent or figure out another work-around.

## Cloning the Image

Because I like to have all my layers available to use as long as possible, it is too early in the painting to collapse everything together. The best work-around is to clone the whole image, copy the entire clone, and paste it back into the original painting. Granted, all the layers are collapsed in the Clone layer, but we also have all the original layers intact should we need them.

1. Clone the painting.

2. Select the whole clone image.

3. Copy the image.

4. Paste the copy of the clone image into the original.

   Continue painting the image.

1. Use the Variable Chalk brush and paint the shadow areas of the character using colors selected from the background. Using background colors in the foreground character helps maintain the color harmonies.

2. Use the same colors from the background but lightened to paint the lighter areas of the sleepwalker.

3. Paint the face and other areas of skin using variations of the violet colors also found in the background.

4. The only area that will need colors that are not already in the painting is the candle. Pick the colors for the candle from the red, orange, and yellow color ranges.

As we paint the character, we are also painting into the background. In Figure 5.11, I have painted over quite a bit of the pattern on the wall. This is not a problem. We will restore the pattern in the finishing touches.

**Figure 5.11** The character is painted in more detail, with attention given to making sure the colors remain harmonious. The sketch is being covered as more color is added.

We can delete the clone image because we do not need it anymore.

5. As you begin to paint details, you should initially paint them on new layers just in case you make a mistake.

The rim lights that I want to paint on the character's face are a good example. If I work in a new layer, I can easily erase errors without consequence to the rest of the painting should these lights not look right. The new layer also gives me a lot of room to experiment. I can try painting the lights everything from very light yellow to deep orange.

6. The colors used to paint the rim lights will be the bright colors of the candle, so you will paint both on the same new layer. Paint the bright colors of the candle first. Using the colors found in the candle, paint rim lights on the edge of the sleepwalker's face, on his hands, and on the part of his nightgown that is closest to the candle (Figure 5.12).

**Figure 5.12** The bright colors of the candle and flame are painted. An orange rim light is painted on the edge of the sleepwalker's face. The light is also painted on his hands and the part of his nightgown closest to the candle.

## Adding Floorboards for Balance

As we paint the figure, the background starts to look a little stark. Adding a floorboard to the junction of the floor and wall gives some weight to the bottom of the image and helps balance the composition. We can create the floorboard using rectangular selections.

1. Create a new layer.

2. Drag a long narrow rectangular selection the width of the painting using the Rectangular Selection tool. The height of the selection is up you.

3.   Using a dark color from one of the corners of the painting, fill in the selection with a number of loose strokes.

4.   Create another layer for the small tops of the floorboard.

5.   Using the Rectangular Selection tool, again drag a short selection the width of the painting.

6.   Paint this selection with a lighter color selected from the wall.

7.   With the selection still active, pick the Layer Adjuster tool. Hold down the Alt key and click-drag a copy of the colored selection slightly above the first.

When we use the Layer Adjuster tool on an active selection, a Layer Floating Object is created. This is not a new layer but a nondestructive copy of the original layer. It's easy to tell we have created one by looking at the Layers palette. There will be an offset preview located under the original layer, and it will be labeled Layer Floating Object.

8.   Move around the Layer Floating Object as much as needed. When it is positioned correctly, use the Layer Commands and drop the Floater onto the layer directly above.

9.   Merge the two Floorboard layers (Figure 5.13).

**Figure 5.13** Floorboards are added to the painting, giving balance and improving the composition.

The floorboard looks a little barren. In fact, the whole left side of the painting is a bit empty, so we will add a small wooden decoration to the floorboard using the same technique we used to draw the floorboards.

1. Create a new layer to add decoration to the floorboard.

2. Draw a roughly square selection on the new layer using the Rectangle Selection tool. Hold down the Shift key to constrain the selection to a square if you want.

3. Paint the selected area with the same color as the larger part of the floorboard.

4. Using the Selection Adjuster tool, scale down the active selection and center it over the just-painted square shape.

5. Paint the second square with the same color used on the thin portions of the floorboards.

6. Using the Oval Selection tool, select a circle on top of the last square.

7. Paint the circle with the same darker color used earlier. Continue the process until you have drawn and painted four additional circles (Figure 5.14).

**Figure 5.14** A small decoration has been painted over the floorboard. It will be finished as the painting progresses.

## Smoothing Out the Rough Spots

The whole image needs some blending to smooth out some of the rougher spots. The best brush for the task, or at least one of my favorite blending brushes, is the Grainy Water 30 variant from the Blenders category. Not only does this brush blend well, but it also interacts with paper textures. Blending leaves some texture behind. It is actually quite a nice combination.

1. Pick the Grainy Water 30 variant from the Blenders brush category.

2. Lower the Opacity setting of the brush to around 20%. Lowering the Opacity setting gives a more subtle blend.

3. Blend a little bit over the entire image. You do not want to obliterate the underlying colors but blend enough to give the impression that you are looking through a soft focus photograph filter (Figure 5.15).

**Figure 5.15** Blending the image to achieve a soft focus appearance

The painting is pretty well set at this point. The color is working, the composition has improved, and a story is even starting to evolve. The finishing touches are not far off.

But the edges of the sleepwalker are pretty rough, so let's clean them up.

1. Pick the Variable Chalk brush.

2. Lower the Opacity setting of the brush to about 25%.

3. Using the brush at a small size and with a dark color picked from one of the corners in the painting, carefully clean up and add an outline to the character.

4. When you are finished, add an outline to the floorboards and possibly some cracks running through them (Figure 5.16).

**Figure 5.16** The edges of the figure are cleaned up, and an outline is added to both the sleepwalker and the floorboards.

## Painting the Eye Candy in the Image

Now that the painting is looking pretty good and the sleepwalker in particular is coming together, it is time to paint a little eye candy in the painting. Actually, the eye candy in this painting is the reason for actually picking this subject.

We will add the burning candle; we've already painted the base colors, but not the glow light. We will also add some smoke coming from the candle. I know, candles do not smoke when they are lit, but this is a fantasy painting, and the candles will do anything I want, including smoking. Finally, we will paint a little moonlight shining through a window onto the wall and the sleepwalker.

All these different objects are great fun to paint and definitely add some sparkle to a digital painting.

### Adding Wispy Smoke

Let's begin by painting some wispy smoke coming from the candle.

1. Create a new layer.
2. Pick the Fine Spray airbrush variant in the Airbrushes category, and paint a wispy and curly plume of smoke coming from the flame (Figure 5.17).
3. Pick the Soften effect and blur the smoke. Set the Amount to 4.
4. Duplicate the curling Smoke layer.
5. Hide the bottom Smoke layer so it's easier to see the changes you're making to the top layer.

**Figure 5.17** A curly plume of smoke is painted on a new layer using the Fine Spray airbrush.

**6.** Pick the Distorto variant in the Distortion brush category.

**7.** In the options bar, change Grain to 12% and Opacity to 0.

**8.** As you paint over the smoke, push and pull with the brush to exaggerate the curly nature of the wisps (Figure 5.18).

**Figure 5.18** The Distorto brush is used to push and pull the painted smoke to exaggerate its wispy appearance.

9. Unhide the lower Smoke layer.

10. Select both Smoke layers and collapse them to one layer (Figure 5.19).

**Figure 5.19** The two Smoke layers are collapsed to one layer.

The smoke looks pretty good. It has a nice transient appearance, but the color is rather boring. It's easy to add color to the smoke by following these steps.

1. Create a new layer above the Smoke layer.

2. Fill the layer with a linear gradient that begins with a blue on the right to an orange on the left.

3. Change the Composite Method of the layer to Colorize.

4. Click on the Smoke layer, and load a selection based on transparency.

5. Invert the selection.

6. Click on the Gradient layer, and press the Backspace key to clear the layer of everything except the area protected by the selection.

7. Select the Gradient layer and Smoke layer and collapse them together.

8. Lower the Opacity setting of the Smoke layer to around 30% (Figure 5.20).

The smoke is finished. It is curly and wispy as expected, and we added some subtle color to make it look more interesting.

**Figure 5.20** A subtle color shift has been added to the smoke.

## Cooling Down the Night

Generally, night scenes are painted in deep blues, and the values are kept darker. Over the course of painting this image, it has become too warm and a bit too light for a night scene. We need to cool the colors and slightly darken the image.

1. Create a new layer.
2. Fill the new layer with a cool blue color.
3. Change the Composite Mode of the layer to Colorize. The whole image is tinted a blue color.
4. Lower the Opacity setting of the Blue layer to between 40% and 50%.
5. Selectively erase around the candle on the Blue layer to remove the color.

There are a few more small painting touches that we still need to do.

1. Merge the floorboards together and paint some shadows into the decorative molding to give it dimension.
2. Redraw and clean up the outline of the sleepwalker.
3. Finish painting the candle and flame. Use the Glow brush to add a subtle glowing area in the atmosphere surrounding the top of the candle and the flame.
4. Using the Glow brush, again paint the candle flame and add highlights to the candleholder.
5. Reveal the two candle Glow layers that have been hidden up to this point.

With the whole image darkened and tinted blue, the Candle Glow layers revealed, and cleanup work painted on both the sleepwalker and the background, the painting is getting very close to being finished (Figure 5.21).

**Figure 5.21** The candle glow has been revealed, and a dark blue tint was added to the sleepwalker, almost finishing the painting.

## Enhancing the Mood with Moonlight

Even though the painting is almost finished, it would be nice to add a few more touches to make the image more interesting. I would like to add a window frame to let in moonlight from the outside. This moonlight will fall across both the sleepwalker and the wall behind him.

With traditional painting media, this type of effect would be a little difficult and time consuming to paint. But the tools available to the digital artist make creating moonlight a pretty simple chore.

To go about adding the effect of moonlight shining through a window and falling across both the sleepwalker and wall, we need to create a window shape.

1. Using the Pen tool, draw the shape of a window in the painting. If you need to reposition the shape you just drew, use the Shape Selection tool to select all the points in the shape and move the whole shape.

2. Convert the shape to a selection using the Convert to Selection command in the Shapes menu.

3. Create a new layer and name it Window.

4. On the new layer, fill the selection with a light greenish color (Figure 5.22).

**Figure 5.22** The shape has been converted into a selection and filled with a light greenish color.

5. Change the Composite Method of the Window layer to Overlay.

6. Duplicate the Window layer once. One layer will be used for the light on the back wall. The copy will be used for the light on the figure.

7. Adjust the Opacity setting of each layer so the effect of the light falling across the figure and background is not too jarring.

8. Using the Layer Adjuster tool, move the layer that will be across the sleepwalker up above the first layer in the image.

We moved up this second layer because the light shining through the window would cross the sleepwalker first and fall across the wall in the background second.

9. Temporarily hide the top layer (the one that will have the light falling across the figure).

10. Using the Eraser brush, carefully erase all the light that is falling across the sleepwalking figure. The light on this layer will fall across the floor and onto the back wall (Figure 5.23).

11. Reveal the top Light layer. Using the Eraser brush, erase any of the layer that is not covering the sleepwalker (Figure 5.24).

**Figure 5.23** Any light falling across the figure is erased.

**Figure 5.24** Those portions of the Light layer not covering the figure are erased.

**12.** Using the Variable Chalk brush along with the Eraser brush, clean up and add curved contours on the layer so the light looks like it is falling across folded fabric (Figure 5.25).

**13.** Apply a slight blur to each layer using Soften from the Effects menu. The default amount is just fine.

**Figure 5.25** The Variable Chalk brush and the Eraser tool add curves to the edges of the Light layer so it appears to be falling across folded fabric.

While the light falling across the figure and wall is not technically accurate, it does give the impression we want. We can use this simple technique to add light to virtually any painting where we want that little bit of extra interest.

We can also use the same technique to create shadows in an image. We would use either Gel or Multiply instead of Overlay as the Composite Method.

## Finishing Touches

A few more small touches, and the painting will be finished. These additions are simple and for the most part do not require a lengthy listing of steps.

- Lighten the skin on the leg of the sleepwalker that is in the moonlight. The leg was rather flat and still about the same color as the front leg. Use the Variable Chalk brush for the small touchup.

- At the last moment, I decide to add a baited mousetrap right in front of the walking figure. This adds a bit of additional story to the painting and is completely optional. Paint the mousetrap on a new layer using the Variable Chalk brush so that you can move it around the image until you find just the right spot to place it.

- Because the mousetrap adds a story line to the painting, I decided to build on that by adding glowing mouse eyes inside the mouse hole on the wall.

You can see all these additions in Figure 5.26.

**Figure 5.26** The leg of the sleepwalker is lightened to give it more dimension, a mousetrap is painted on a new layer right in front of the character, and mouse eyes are painted in the mouse hole.

Just two more steps and the painting will be finished.

To be safe, we'll apply the last two steps to a clone of the image. I do this because I want to keep the original layered image intact just in case any changes or revisions need to be made in the future.

1. Clone the image. You can save and close the original. You don't need it anymore.

2. Using the Apply Surface Texture effect in the Effects > Surface Control menu, apply a subtle texture over the whole image. Use the paper texture we've been using all along with the Variable Chalk brush, but make the following changes to the default settings in the Apply Surface Texture options box:

   - Set the Shine slider to zero (0).
   - Set the Amount slider to 20%.

Eliminating shine is an obvious option because the surface does not need to look wet or shiny. Lowering the Amount enhances the painted strokes instead of overpowering them, as would have happened at 100%.

The whole image now looks like it was painted with some sort of pastel tool on a sheet of textured paper (Figure 5.27).

**Figure 5.27** A close-up of the painting shows the subtle surface texture that was applied to the whole image.

The final step is to apply a lighting effect one last time.

3. Select Apply Lighting from the Effects > Surface control menu with the default lighting scheme Warm Globe.

4. Click the OK button in the Apply Lighting box to apply the effect. The overall tone of the painting is lowered slightly, and the colors are subdued. This last effect is perfect to finish off the painting (Figure 5.28).

**Figure 5.28** The finished painting with the lighting effect applied

# Final Thoughts

I hope that you were able to pick up some important techniques to use in your own work in the future. In this chapter, you should have learned the following lessons:

- How to paint a light source. In this case, we worked with a candle, but you would apply many of the same steps if you were painting a lightbulb, campfire, lit match, or really any small light source you would want to add to a painting.

- A way to paint smoke that, while not necessarily accurate to the way smoke looks in real life, is nevertheless effective when used in an illustration.

- How to paint a night scene and manage the values and colors to give a believable feel without creating a dull, gray image.

- How to paint the impression of moonlight shining through a window and falling both on the character and wall.

# Painting a Sea Serpent

*I have a fondness for sea and lake monsters. The Loch Ness monster in particular is one of my favorites. It really doesn't matter to me whether sea serpents exist or not; just the idea of them is so attractive. Every so often, I paint one just for the heck of it. Of all the paintings in this book, this is probably the one that I did mostly for the fun of it.*

*While this is not the most technical of all the paintings in the book as far as specific tricks and features used to create it, it's helpful to demonstrate the many techniques that I used to speed up the painting process immeasurably. I've already described some of these techniques in earlier chapters. However, it does not hurt to revisit them again to make sure you understand the process.*

**Chapter Contents**

## Using a Paper Texture for the Image

This painting is based on a sketch from one of my sketchbooks. I drew the sketch on 110-pound cover stock paper with a black grape Prismacolor pencil. I like to draw on heavyweight cover stock because it takes a lot of abuse and generally has a very nice surface on which to sketch. The black grape Prismacolor pencil is a nice dark, somewhat gray, violet color.

I scanned the original sketch at 300 dpi (dots per inch) for this tutorial. I reduced the image to about half of the original scanned size. Reducing the size was mainly for convenience when working with the image and because I generally knew how large the image would be printed.

 **Note:** The scanned sketch is available for download at www.sybex.com/go/painter.

### Creating the Paper Texture

The first thing we need to do before we begin painting is create a paper texture that will be used as the base texture in the painting. The paper that this sketch was originally drawn on has a nice organic texture, and I want to use this texture in the painting. There are several ways to do this. I could build a texture by selecting some of the scanned sketch and repeatedly pasting copies until the whole canvas is covered, but an easier and less time-consuming solution is to scan a blank sheet of the same paper that I drew the image on. I've opted for the second solution and have scanned a whole sheet of the same type of paper.

Normally I would take the image of the scanned paper and make it a seamless texture. In this case, though, the seams formed at the edges of the scan are not very noticeable, so I'm not going to worry about making a seamless texture.

1.  Scan a blank sheet of paper and then simply create a pattern to use in the painting by selecting the Capture Pattern command from the Patterns palette.

2.  Select the entire image and create a paper texture using the Capture Paper command in the Papers palette.

Now there's a paper texture and a pattern to use in the image that is similar to the texture in the original sketch.

 **Note:** Both the pattern and paper texture are available for download at www.sybex.com/go/painter.

3.  Open the sketch in Painter. Initially, you want the drawing to be on its own layer, so select the entire image using the Ctrl+A (⌘+A on the Mac) keyboard

combination, cut the image using Ctrl+X (⌘+X on the Mac), and paste it back into itself using Ctrl+V (⌘+V on the Mac). The Canvas has now been cleared, and the image is now on a new layer.

4.    The drawing crowds the edges of the scan, so add more space around the sketch using the Canvas Size command from the Canvas menu. The total size of the image is now about 1,900 pixels wide and 1,000 pixels tall. The exact size is not critical, and you could have added more or less. Figure 6.1 shows the sketch with additional space around the drawing created by the Canvas Size command.

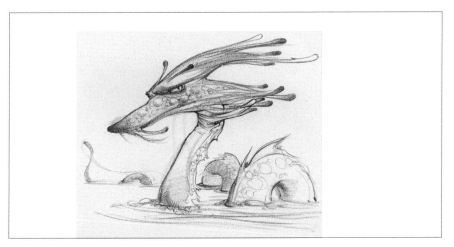

**Figure 6.1**  Additional space is created around the drawing using the Canvas Size command.

5.    Select the pattern created from the scanned paper, and fill the Canvas layer with the paper texture using the Paint Bucket tool. If the background is filled with a color or gradient instead of the paper pattern, make sure you select Clone Source from the Options bar when you select the Paint Bucket tool. Figure 6.2 shows the sketch with the Canvas layer filled with the paper pattern.

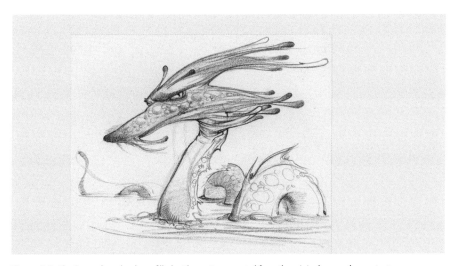

**Figure 6.2**  The Canvas layer has been filled with a pattern created from the original scanned paper texture.

6. Duplicate the Sketch layer. Make sure the Duplicated layer is active, and click the small padlock icon to lock the layer so you don't accidentally draw or paint on the layer. You will use this layer only as a reference if you need to come back to the original sketch later in the painting. Click the eye icon to hide the layer.

The original Sketch layer is now dropped onto the canvas.

7. Pick Don's Digital Water 2 brush and, using greens, blues, violets, and browns, paint over the entire image to set the color and value of the painting.

I use this watercolor brush when I want to add color to an image without covering the original sketch. The colors mingle and blend with each other in a way similar to traditional watercolor. Selecting a lighter color actually paints the lighter color back into the image, unlike traditional watercolor. For this reason, it's a great brush to use when experimenting with the colors in a painting; it's easy to make color corrections. I use this brush and variations of it extensively in the early stages of paintings. I sometimes even set it so it will interact with my paper textures.

My goal is not to set the final colors of the painting at this point but merely to set the mood and cover the surface so I'm not painting on the bright canvas. Figure 6.3 shows the painting after using the watercolor brush to cover the whole surface. Notice where I used lighter colors and painted them back into the body of the sea monster.

**Figure 6.3** The whole canvas has been painted over using a digital watercolor brush to set the mood and get rid of the bright canvas.

## Wet and Dry Digital Watercolor Layers

One characteristic of using a digital watercolor brush that can be both a pleasure and a pain is that the painted watercolor remains wet. Now, of course, it's not really wet, but it acts in a way that is quite different from most other brushes. At any time, we can come back with a digital watercolor brush and paint into the surface; the colors mix as if we were painting in wet paint!

Because the digital watercolor paint stays wet indefinitely, we cannot layer our strokes as we would if we were using traditional watercolor and painting over a dry Watercolor layer. If we want to layer our strokes, we must first go to the Layers menu and select Dry Digital Watercolor. The interesting thing is that digital watercolor does not actually create itself a new layer like the regular watercolor brushes, but we still need to use the Layers menu to dry the colors. We can now build up transparent layers of digital watercolor, though we must remember to dry the paint each time we want to start a new layer.

Another characteristic of digital watercolors is they do not react or interact with regular brushes. For example, we cannot use a blending brush on areas painted with digital watercolor. The blender has no effect. If we want regular brushes to interact with digital watercolor, we must also dry the layer again.

The most important thing to remember is that when using digital watercolor, even though it does not create a new layer, it acts as if it is painting on a new layer. Making changes or painting into that digital watercolor requires drying the Digital Watercolor layer.

## Painting the Sea Monster

We're now going to start painting on the sea monster. As in other chapters, we will do this on a new layer just in case we don't like the results or want to be able to make corrections easily.

Eventually we'll do a lot of work to the monster to make him scaly and wet looking, as expected of a typical sea monster. However, we'll add these details toward the end the painting process. This is only a sketch right now, and we need to paint more of the sea monster's character and additional details. The detailing will be a rather experimental process.

When I originally drew the sketch, it was rough. I never thought about the details since I really didn't know that I was going to be painting him.

1. Create a new layer. Also, make sure that the Pickup Underlying Color box is checked.

2. Choose the Pixel Spray airbrush from the Airbrushes category. This is the default brush in Painter.

3. Lower the Opacity setting of the brush to 10%, and set Size to about 3.

### Moving from Dark to Light

Beginning with dark colors and working from the edges of the sketch, I begin painting the sea monster. I use Pixel Spray airbrush at a lower Opacity setting so I can build the colors and textures of the beast, slowly allowing individual colors to mix with underlying color. I select most of my colors from within the image at this early stage. This helps me maintain a color harmony that is sometimes hard to acquire and maintain when constantly going to the Colors palette. Even though I am selecting my colors from within the image, I will go to the Colors palette to lighten or darken them as needed. Right now there's not a very wide range of value in the painting. Things are mostly on the darker side.

I am mostly concerned with refining the profile and edges of the sea monster. I also start to paint some lighter colors into his body, aiming for a kind of bumpy and scaly surface. Figure 6.4 shows the early stages of the painting using the Pixel Spray airbrush to refine the drawing and start building the form.

**Figure 6.4** The early stages of drawing and painting the sea serpent

## Painting in the Details

I add the golden color to the eye of the monster and paint a small vertical pupil over the gold. I'm still using the same Pixel Spray airbrush, painting on the same layer, and having a great time adding more and more detail. I mention this because there is always a danger when you're painting to get too involved in the details at the expense of the overall image. So while I'm going to try to add lots of detail, I will also try to remember that the overall impact of the piece should not be sacrificed for the smaller and less important details. Figure 6.5 shows the sea monster with his eye painted and detail in his head and neck. If I'm not careful, I will overdo it.

**Figure 6.5** I paint the eye and start to get carried away with details in the head and neck. Hopefully it will not be too much.

It should be noted that as I paint the monster, I also paint in the background to help me clean up the edges and refine his shape. When I do this, I paint over some of the original texture in the background. This is not a problem because I will put it back later in the painting.

I'm at a point in the painting where most of the original sketch is covered. I've added a tail and fins to the monster's humps. I'm pretty happy with the overall look of the monster, and I don't think I've overdone the detail. I'm still only using the Pixel Spray airbrush for all the painting. So far in the painting, I've used only two brushes. Sometimes when working on a painting, it is better not to use all the available features. Sometimes less is more, and the simplest approach is the best (Figure 6.6).

**Figure 6.6** The sea serpent is coming right along, and all the work in the painting has been done with only two brushes. Sometimes the simplest approach is the best.

Because my sea serpent is a reptile of sorts, I want to add scales to his body. Painting scales individually can be a tedious process, and most of us would not have the patience to attempt doing this. Fortunately, there are several easy ways to add scales to our monster using patterns or paper textures.

A set of premade reptile paper textures and patterns is available for download at www.sybex.com/go/painter. It is a good idea, though, to go ahead and make a new paper texture and a new pattern so that you understand the process and can make additional libraries for yourself.

First, we need to create a scaly-looking paper texture. There is an often-overlooked feature in Painter that makes creating this type of texture extremely easy. This feature is found in the Canvas menu and is called Make Tessellation.

To create a scaly paper texture, we will do the following:

1. Create a new image that is approximately 600 pixels by 600 pixels. I usually find that creating a square paper texture works best.

2. In the Colors palette, select a mid-value to slightly lighter than mid-value color.

3. From the Canvas menu, select the Make Tessellation command.

**4.** The Make Tessellation options box opens (Figure 6.7).

**5.** In the Make Tessellation box, you're presented with several drop-down menus. In the Options box, select Add 500 Evenly Spaced Points. In the Display drop-down menu, you have several options.

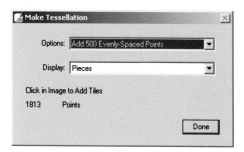

**Figure 6.7** The Make Tessellation options box

We can base the tessellation on Triangles, Cracks, or Pieces. Generally, I find the triangles do not work very well for what I'm trying to do, so we will use either the Cracks or Pieces option. If we choose Pieces, the size of the individual elements will vary from small to large pieces. If we choose Cracks, the size of the individual elements will be relatively uniform.

For creating a reptile skin pattern, it really will not matter if we choose cracks or pieces.

**6.** Choose the Pieces option, and a preview image of a series of lines will appear in your new image.

Figure 6.8 shows how the image would be divided into 500 evenly spaced points using the Make Tessellation command.

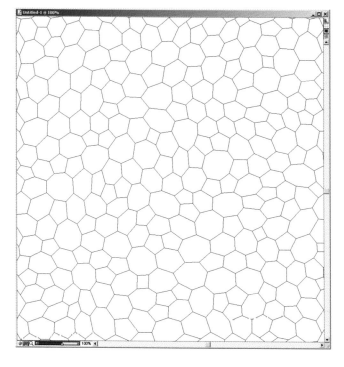

**Figure 6.8** Results of dividing an image into 500 evenly spaced points

If at this point we click Done, 500 evenly spaced points based on cracks will be added to the image. But we actually want the pattern to be a bit more complicated and have more scaly pieces.

7.   Go to the Options menu and select Add 500 Evenly Spaced Points four additional times. Each time you select the option, another 500 points are added to the image.

8.   Click the Done button. The individual pieces are drawn as white lines on a colored background. The color of the background is whatever color you selected in step 2.

Figure 6.9 shows the image divided when we click the Done button. The pattern is now much more complicated and has a nice scaly feel about it.

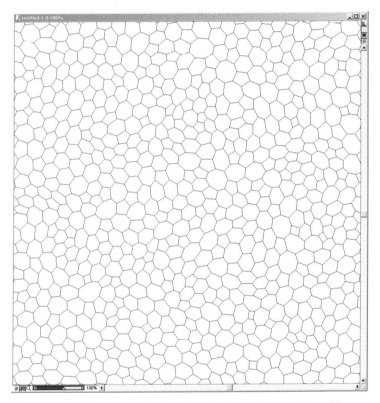

**Figure 6.9**   The divided image after choosing Add 500 Evenly Spaced Points an additional four times

## Making the Scales Seamless

Unfortunately, the image we just created is not a seamless texture. If we used this image without making it a seamless texture, we would see seams at the edges where the pattern does not line up. So we need to take some time and make this reptile texture seamless.

1.   In the Patterns palette, from the Patterns menu, select Define Pattern. You will notice in the preview window that the new reptile texture immediately becomes visible.

2. Hold down the Spacebar and Shift keys. In the image window, your cursor has become a small hand. Click and drag in the image. Notice as you drag in the image that the edges of the pattern become visible as broken lines or rough and uneven edges. Drag until you have the vertical and horizontal edges in the center of the image.

Here's where the work will become a little bit tedious.

3. Select Dons brush, and along with the Eraser, clean up and join the broken lines. Extreme accuracy is not important; what you're trying to do is get rid of the broken lines you can see in the image. Eventually when you paint and use this as a texture or pattern, you will not be able to tell where you made any of the corrections if you're careful.

Figure 6.10 shows a before and after comparison of the images. The left side of the image is before the seams were fixed, and the right side shows the same image with the seams painted.

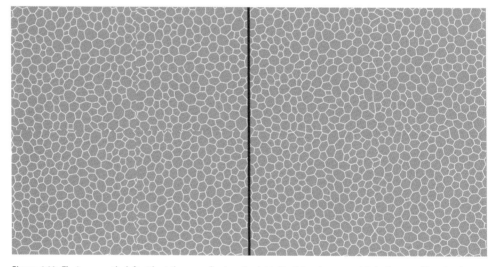

**Figure 6.10** The image on the left without the seams fixed; on the right after fixing the seams with the Eraser and Dons brush

The lines in the image are crisp and sharp. A paper texture generally gives better results if there are no harsh edges. So we will slightly soften the lines in our texture using the Soften effect.

4. From the Effects menu, select the Soften command. The Aperture should have Gaussian checked, and the Amount should be set to approximately 4. Click OK.

5. Invert the lights and darks in the texture using the Effects > Tonal Control >, Negative menu.

The only real reason I invert the texture is to get a better sense of how it will look as a scaly pattern. The space between scales is generally darker than the scales themselves, and this lets me see the effect better.

There's one last step, and the texture will be ready to make into a paper and pattern.

6. From the menu, select the Highpass command found in the Esoterica group of effects. With the Highpass options box open; check Circular, and set the Amount to 11.5. Click OK.

A slightly darker center has been added to each of the cells in our texture. This is done to add a bit more dimension to the painting when using this specific texture.

7. Select the entire image using Ctrl+A.

8. From the menu in the Papers palette, select Capture Paper.

9. Name your paper `Reptile Skin` or some other descriptive name, and set the Crossfade to 0 since the texture is already seamless. Click OK.

The new paper is saved in the default paper library and becomes the active paper. We know it is the active paper because we can see a preview of it in the Papers palette.

Usually, when I create a paper texture, if the texture has been made from a color image, I also save it as a pattern. Patterns can be very useful because they use the color information, whereas a paper pattern does not.

10. From the Patterns menu in the Patterns palette, select Capture Pattern. Name your pattern, leave Rectangular Tile checked, and leave Bias set to 0. Click OK.

You now have a pretty convincing reptile texture saved as both a paper and a pattern.

## Practicing Scales

Before we actually add scales to the dragon, we want to go through the procedure in a new image so it is clear and easily understandable. In this example, I will also use one of the reptile textures that I created earlier and that is available for download at `www.sybex.com/go/painter` instead of the texture we just created.

1. Begin by creating a new image. The actual size of the image does not matter, but try something in the 600- to 900-pixel range.

2. Since you are painting a reptile, go ahead and fill the test image with the mid-value green color.

3. Choose the Variable Chalk brush. You can find this brush in the Chalk brush category. In the Brush Property bar at the top of the screen, lower the Grain slider to about 6%.

4. Pick a darker green color, make sure you have a reptile paper texture active, and paint the scales in the new image. Figure 6.11 shows the darker scales painted using the Chalk brush.

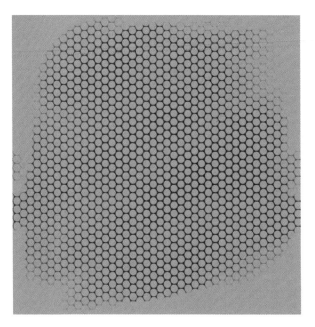

**Figure 6.11** shows darker scales painted using the Variable Chalk brush.

Now that the darker edges of the scales are painted, let's add some lighter color between the dark scales.

**5.** In the Papers palette, invert the paper texture by pressing the Invert Paper button (Figure 6.12). Figure 6.12 shows the location of the Invert Paper button on the Papers palette.

**Figure 6.12** The Invert Paper button

**6.** Choose a lighter green color from the Colors palette.

**7.** Increase the Grain amount to 10%.

**8.** Use the Variable Chalk brush to paint lighter scales into the image (Figure 6.13). Finally, we will add some highlights to the edges of the scales.

**9.** Once again, set the Grain slider to 6%.

**10.** Pick an even lighter green color than you used in step 6 and paint highlights on the scales once again using the Variable Chalk brush (Figure 6.14).

Notice that when I got toward the edges of the image, I did not need to paint a complete scale using the dark color, a lighter color, and the highlight color to have the effect read as reptile scales. This is an important concept to remember as we continue to paint on the sea serpent. It's not necessary to paint every little detail to have the viewer see what's intended. As I paint more into the sea serpent, I will use this idea; in some areas I paint only dark edges of the scales, while in other areas I paint only the lighter portion of the scales. This keeps the repetitive texture from becoming monotonous.

Now that I've explained how to create a paper texture and a pattern that looks like reptile skin and how to use the paper pattern to paint the effect of scales in an image, it's time to add some scales to the sea serpent.

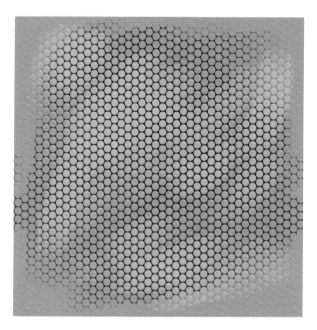

**Figure 6.13** The lighter scales have been painted into the image.

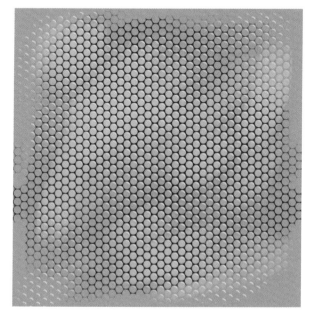

**Figure 6.14** An image that looks like reptile skin painted quickly and easily using a ustom paper texture

### Adding Scales to the Sea Serpent

Now we are ready to add scales to the sea serpent. We need to load the Reptile Paper library from the Papers palette.

1. Click on the Palette menu arrow in the upper-right corner of the Papers palette.

2. From the menu, select Open Library. In the option box that opens, select the Append button. If you choose to Load instead of Append, make sure that you have backed up any custom paper textures you have created.

Loading a paper library instead of appending the new textures into our current active library erases all the current paper textures. Because the Reptile Paper Texture library is relatively small, we should just append these textures to the open library.

Of course, another alterative is to use custom-created paper textures.

 **Note:** The reptile paper library is available for download at www.sybex.com/go/painter.

We painted the earlier demonstration image in this chapter on the Canvas layer. Unlike that image, we'll paint the scales added in this painting on separate layers. There will be an individual layer for the dark scales and the light scales. We won't be worried about adding highlights to the scales in this image.

With the sea serpent image open

1. Create two new layers. Label one layer dark scales and the other light scales.

2. Check the Pick Up Underlying Color box if it is not already checked.

3. Choose the Variable Chalk brush, and lower the Grain to 6% in the Brush property bar at the top of the screen.

4. Select one of the darker colors from within those painted on the sea serpent. Carefully paint dark scales on the monster. Use varying pressure, and do not paint completely uniform scales across the whole creature.

5. Using the Scale slider in the Papers palette, vary the size of the scales being painted. Keep the larger scales in the larger areas of the creature's body, and use smaller scales in the smaller areas such as the face and head. Figure 6.15 shows larger scales painted into the body of the sea serpent, with smaller scales on the belly and the face.

6. Use the Eraser tool to vary the Opacity setting of the painted scales in different areas of the body. You do not need to have a solid layer of scales painted to give the impression of a scaly surface.

7. Switch to the Light Scale layer. Select one of the lighter colors from within the serpent, and paint some lighter scales over the creature. Do not worry if the scales fill up and cover the darker scales. Using the Eraser tool and the Opacity setting of the layer, you can adjust the scales until they fit visually. Figure 6.16

shows the scales painted without adjusting the Opacity setting or erasing into the layer.

8. Using the Eraser tool, go into the Light Scale layer and erase any areas where you do not want light scales to show.

**Figure 6.15** Dark scales are painted onto a new layer over the sea serpent. Larger scales are painted over the body, and smaller scales are painted over the belly and head of the creature.

**Figure 6.16** Lighter scales painted on a new layer over the darker scales.

Usually, I erase the scales where they overlap the darker and shadowed areas of the figure. Figure 6.17 shows the earlier image with some of the lighter scales erased in the shadow areas.

**Figure 6.17** Some of the scales on a lighter layer are erased where they overlap the darker shadows in the serpent.

If the scales are still distracting because they're too noticeable, we can lower the Opacity setting of the layer.

Usually a more subtle look with the scales is better than something so obvious that it's distracting. There is no standard amount of Opacity reduction to suggest because every individual's image will look different. Just find what works best with the painting.

9. Continue painting the scales on the sea serpent, but don't paint too many. Do that and you run the risk of making the painting look mechanical and contrived.

The sea serpent is looking pretty good so far. But when I think of sea serpents, I often envision a misty or foggy environment where the creature suddenly appears as it silently swims through the water. Thick fog is also kind of spooky in its own right.

In the next section, we will add some fog to the painting and make the monster silently emerge from it.

## Adding the Fog Bank

Adding a fog bank to the painting gives a feeling of mystery to the scene. Adding fog is not difficult, but it does involve quite a few simple steps. The effort is worth it, though, because the fog adds so much visually to the painting.

To add a layer of fog, we must first create an entirely new image using the Make Fractal Pattern command from the Patterns palette.

1.  Create a fractal pattern that is 512×512 pixels in size. A pattern with smaller dimensions than this will not scale well for use in this image.

We also want the texture in the pattern to be large and relatively soft since we are going to be imitating a fog bank.

2.  When you have the Make Fractal Pattern options box visible, you can either experiment until you get something you think will work or simply use these settings for the sliders (Figure 6.18):

    •  Power: –138%

    •  Feature Size: 31%

    •  Softness: 69%

    •  Angle: 0

    •  Thinness: 100%

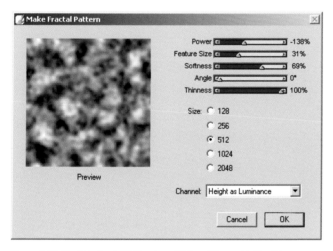

**Figure 6.18**  The Make Fractal Pattern box with the settings set to the sliders

3.  Click OK to exit the options box and create a new image.

The fractal pattern just created really does not look anything like fog. In the next few steps, we'll transform this black-and-white square into a convincing fog bank. The first thing we need to do is to get this fractal pattern we just created into our sea serpent picture.

1.  Select the entire fractal pattern image.

2.  Copy or cut the image and paste it into the sea serpent painting (Figure 6.19).

The fractal pattern image can be closed. We will not need it anymore. We can save the image when we close it or opt not to.

3.  Lower the Opacity setting of this new layer to around 85%.

**Figure 6.19** The fractal pattern image is pasted into the sea serpent painting in preparation for transforming it into a fog bank.

The amount is not critical; we just want to get a slight bit of transparency to the image so when we transform it, we have a little better idea of what we're doing.

4. In the Effects menu at the top of the screen, select Orientation and then Free Transform. Using the handles that appear at the corners and in the middle of each of the sides of the fractal pattern, scale the pattern so it covers almost the entire painting in the horizontal dimension.

5. Right-click the layer and select Commit to accept the transform and change the layer back to a default layer.

6. Move the layer up or down, depending on where the original layer is pasted into the painting. The bottom of the layer should be at about the same height as where the sea serpent's tail enters the water (Figure 6.20).

7. Change the Composite Method of the layer to Screen. All the black in the layer becomes transparent, or nearly so.

**Figure 6.20** The Fractal Pattern layer is scaled with the Free Transform tool so it covers almost the entire horizontal area of the painting. The layer is also moved so that the bottom is at the same height as the sea serpent's tail entering the water.

8.    Erase the hard edges of the layer so you have soft edges around the entire layer's perimeter.

9.    Lower the Opacity setting of the layer to about 40% (Figure 6.21).

**Figure 6.21** With the Composite Method of the layer changed to Screen, the hard edges erased until they are soft, and the Opacity setting of the entire layer lowered to 40%, the Fractal Pattern layer starts to look quite a bit like a fog bank.

10.   From the Layers menu, load a selection based on the transparency of this Fog layer.

11.   With the selection active, create a new layer.

12.   Use the Digital airbrush and paint the fog a dark green color on the new layer.

The extent of where we are able to paint is constrained by the active selection. Most of the color goes on top of our clouds.

13.   Change the Composite Method of this Painted layer to Color. The fog bank has now taken on a nice greenish tint.

14.   Select the original black-and-white Fog layer. Change its Composite Method back to the default.

15.   Select both the top Color layer and the bottom Fog layer, and collapse the two into one layer.

16.   Change the Composite Method of this new layer back to Screen.

17.   Lower the Opacity setting of the layer to about 45%.

18.   Duplicate the layer. Label the bottom layer Back Fog and the top layer Front Fog.

19.   Temporarily hide the Front Fog layer.

20.   Using the Free Transform command, extend the Back Fog layer until it covers the entire width of the image. Right-click the layer to commit the transform.

21.   Use the Eraser tool to clear off any of the fog that is covering the front two sections of the sea monster (Figure 6.22).

22.   Reveal the Front Fog layer.

**Figure 6.22** The Fog layer covering the front two sections of the sea monster has been erased, leaving the remaining sections of the sea monster gradually appearing out of the fog.

**23.** Using the Free Transform command again, scale the Front Fog layer both higher and wide enough to cover the entire image. Commit to transform.

**24.** Lower the Opacity setting of the Front Fog layer to 30%.

**25.** Use the Eraser tool to clear any of the Front Fog layer that is covering the first three sections of the sea serpent. This leaves the last two humps of the monster covered by two layers of fog, the third hump covered by one layer of fog, and the front hump and neck not covered by any fog (Figure 6.23).

**Figure 6.23** The fog bank is finished.

We'll save the painting in preparation for our next step, which will be adding the sea serpent's reflection in the water. We'll drop all the layers to the canvas and save the image again using the Iterative Save feature. To make the reflections work in the next section, we need to be working with an image that's just the Canvas layer.

## Adding the Sea Serpent's Reflection in the Water

To add a reflection of the sea serpent in the water, we will use a slightly different technique than presented in Chapter 2, "Painting Clouds, Water, and Stone." The new technique is actually a bit easier and the results, in my opinion, are very cool and just as effective.

Because the sea monster is positioned so low in the picture plane, we will not be able to see a complete reflection, so we won't be able to include his head. This actually simplifies the problem a bit since we won't need to deal with the complexities of getting the head reflection looking good.

Let's begin.

1. Use the Rectangular Selection tool and drag a selection around the entire lower half of the painting from the tip of the tail to the bottom of the image.

2. Copy and paste the selection back into the image.

3. Using Effects > Orientation > Flip Vertical, flip the whole selection along its vertical axis.

4. Using the Lasso tool, select the tail and last hump of the sea serpent on the new layer.

5. Copy and paste the selection into a new layer. The new layer contains only the tail and last hump.

We now have two layers. One layer is the entire lower half of the image, and the other layer, copied from the first, is only the tail and the last hump of the sea serpent. Both these layers are flipped vertically from the original image.

6. Using the Free Transform command, scale both of the new layers until they are about 50% of their original size in the vertical dimension. Right-click and commit both layers back to default layers.

7. In the Patterns palette, select the Water pattern.

**Note:** The water pattern is in the pattern library that is available to download at www.sybex.com/go/painter.

8. With the larger of the two layers active, select from the Effects > Focus > Glass Distortion. In the options box that appears, use the following settings (Figure 6.24).
   - Using: Original Luminance
   - Softness: 4.3
   - Map: Refraction
   - Quality: Good
   - Amount: 2.16
   - Variance: 1.81
   - Direction: 0°

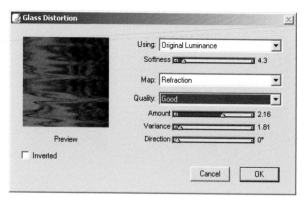

**Figure 6.24** Settings for the Glass Distortion menu.

9.  Click OK to apply the effect to the active layer. The layer now looks like a reflection in water.

10. Apply the same effect to the second layer.

With the reflection-like effect applied to both layers, the painting now looks a lot more like a sea serpent swimming in the water (Figure 6.25).

**Figure 6.25** A water-like effect applied to both layers imitates the reflection of the creature on a watery surface.

11. Choose each layer individually, and from the Effects menu, select Soften. Leave the slider to the default amount of 3, and click OK.

12. Using the Eraser tool, go back to each layer and erase the reflections that cover some of the lower parts of the monster.

You may need to lower the Opacity setting of each layer as you work so that you can see the bottom edge of the original monster. When you're finished erasing, you can raise the Opacity setting back to 100%.

13. Save the image, and drop multiple layers on the canvas. After you've dropped the layers onto the Canvas layer, use the Iterative Save feature and save the file once again.

That's all there is to this technique of adding simple reflections under an object. I need to add some finishing details to the water like waves and wakes caused by his motion. These are easy to paint and will add interest to the water area.

1.  Use Dons brush to paint some waves and wakes caused by the sea serpent moving in the water. Also, paint some larger scales on the first hump.

2.  Refine and paint more detail into the back fin on each of the humps and tail. The amount of detail you paint is completely up to you.

There is no right or wrong stopping point. The painting should now look something like Figure 6.26.

**Figure 6.26** Some waves and wakes have been painted into the reflections, and more detail has been added to the monster.

We're getting pretty close to finishing the painting, but there are a few more small details to add before we're done.

Because this is a dark and murky scene, I am going to add a little moon in the sky. This is easy to do and takes only a few steps, but it will add greatly to the look and feel of the image.

To add a sense of the time of day or at least how dark the environment is I will add a small moon to the upper left corner of the painting. To do this, follow these steps:

1.  Create a new layer in the image.

2.  Using the Oval Selection tool and holding down the Shift key, click and drag a small circular selection on the new layer.

3.  Use the Paint Bucket tool with a color selected from one of the lighter areas in the painting, and fill the circular selection on the new layer.

4.  Change the Composite Method of the new layer to Screen.

5.  Deselect the circle using Ctrl+D.

6.  Use the Soften effect with a setting of 15 to blur the moon.

7.  Lower the Opacity setting of the Moon layer to about 65%.

8.  Use the Eraser and a couple of soft horizontal lines through the moon to simulate clouds passing in front of it.

9. If you are satisfied with the position of the moon in the painting, go ahead and drop it onto the Canvas layer. If you want to change the moon's position, move it anywhere you want using the Layer Adjuster tool.

That's all there is to creating a simple moon (Figure 6.27).

**Figure 6.27** The painting with a simple moon added in the upper-left corner. The addition of this moon adds a whole new level of depth and interest to the painting.

## Finishing Touches

There are really only a couple of things left to do to finish the painting of the sea serpent.

Because he is swimming around in the ocean, we need to add a few intense highlights to make him look wet. This is easily done on a new layer or on the Canvas layer if you're confident with your abilities.

1. Choose Dons brush and a light, slightly greenish color to paint some intense highlights on the closest parts of the sea monster. Do not paint too many, as it is easy to overdo the effect (Figure 6.28).

**Figure 6.28** A few bright and intense highlights have been added on a new layer to give the sea serpent a wet look.

2. When you are happy with the placement of the highlights on the new layer, drop the layer onto the canvas. Make sure you save the image.

3. Pick the Glow brush from the F-X category, choose a bright red color, and carefully paint a bit of glow to the sea serpent's eye.

4. The final touch to finish the painting is to add a lighting effect found in Effects > Surface Control > Apply Lighting. When the options box opens, choose the third lighting scheme called Splashy Color, leave all the default settings alone, and click OK.

The lighting effect is applied to the image, making it darker, adding a nice transition of color from warmer on the left to cooler on the right, and increasing the saturation of the whole painting slightly. The painting is finished (Figure 6.29).

**Figure 6.29** The finished painting of the sea serpent

## Final Thoughts

While this painting was not a particularly complicated piece, it still presented you with several important techniques.

You made a paper texture that you could use to simulate the scaled surface of a reptile. You then were able to use the paper texture in conjunction with various layers to carefully apply a texture to the sea serpent's body. The most important part of this exercise was learning how to use individual layers to control the effect.

You also saw an alternative way of creating a reflection of an object in a watery surface. This technique is in many ways easier than the one presented earlier in the chapter, yet the results of both are similar. It is good when you learn a new application to see various ways of arriving at the same end; I hope this revelation will encourage you to seek out different techniques.

Finally, you saw a technique for creating a fog bank. You can also use this technique to create other weather-related effects, including rain and snow storms.

I hope that you will take what you've learned here and expand upon it while painting your own images.

# Red Riding Hood

*The painting for this tutorial is based on the fairytale Little Red Riding Hood and is pretty straightforward. Most of the tutorial will take place in the painting of the background.*

*A combination of techniques is used to paint the dense undergrowth in the background. This includes the creative use of paper textures, patterns, custom brushes, and the image hose. Some of these techniques were demonstrated individually in earlier chapters, but this chapter combines them to paint the background on which the heroine does her thing.*

*Red herself is simply painted using just a few brushes. There really is no special technique used to paint the main character.*

**Chapter Contents**

## Importing the Sketch and Setting Up the Image

This painting of Red Riding Hood is based on a sketch I did several years ago. Occasionally I get in a fairytale mood, and usually, I add some sort of twist to the original fairytale. In this particular case, Little Red Riding Hood is not nearly the helpless maiden she is in the story. I added a large gun that she must've had discreetly tucked into her cape. Of course, a gun is way too big for dear Red Riding Hood, but that's part of the fun.

The original sketch was scanned at 300 dpi (dots per inch), which made it approximately 5,000 pixels in height. I find this size too large to work on comfortably, so I reduced the size to around 1,500 or 2,000 pixels in the largest dimension. This size makes it easier to paint quickly in the early stages. Then I can gradually increase the size to add details as I finish the image.

 **Note:** The scanned sketch is available for download at www.sybex.com/go/painter.

1. Open the sketch in Painter, and put the drawing on its own layer by selecting the entire image using the Ctrl+A keyboard combination.

2. Cut the image using Ctrl+X, and paste it back into itself using Ctrl+V.

3. With the sketch layer active, use the Effects > Tonal Control > Equalize command to remove most of the grays from the image.

I'm not so worried about any gray in the sketch itself, but we want to make sure that the background areas of the sketch are white so that when we change the layer's Composite Method to Multiply or Gel, these areas will become transparent and not create a gray tint over the colors we paint.

4. Change the Composite Method of the new Sketch layer to Multiply so that all the white in the image becomes transparent.

5. Select the whole image again, make sure the Canvas layer is the active layer, and press the Backspace key to clear the sketch from the bottom Canvas layer.

Figure 7.1 shows the original sketch.

The whole background will be filled with dense undergrowth and a lot of plants. It will be much easier to cover the background with plants and shrubs if we work on top of a green color and don't worry about making sure the Canvas layer doesn't show through what we're painting. Red Riding Hood herself will be standing on a gravel path.

6. Fill the Canvas layer with a gradient starting with a dark green color at the top of the image and ending with a tan color at the bottom. Using the default Digital airbrush, block in the basic colors of Red Riding Hood.

**Figure 7.1** The original
Red Riding Hood sketch

This is going to be a fun painting because of the complementary color scheme. But having a bright red figure on a very green background poses its own unique set of challenges. We have to carefully think out the colors as we paint them. I will try to make sure that I get some colors from the red figure into a green background. If I don't do this, there is a chance that the figure will become so isolated from the background that it does not look like it should be part of the painting. Figure 7.2 shows the sketch with the Canvas layer filled using a gradient and Red Riding Hood's colors quickly painted in.

7.   Duplicate the Sketch layer in case you need to refer back to it somewhere later in the painting.

8.   Click the padlock icon so you do not accidentally paint on this layer, and then click the eye icon to hide the layer.

(As the painting progresses and it's no longer necessary to refer back to the sketch, I will delete this layer.)

9.   The painting feels a little tight on the left side. To add room, go to the Canvas menu and select Canvas Size. When the options box appears, add 250 pixels to the left side of the painting.

10.  The added space is white, so go ahead and fill it with the same gradient used to fill the background. If the original green and tan colors are not still the active colors, simply select them from the top and bottom of the background using the Dropper tool.

**Figure 7.2** A linear gradient ramping from green at the top to tan at the bottom has filled the background, and the basic colors of Red Riding Hood are painted.

We have finished the basic preparation of the image. We have chosen a color scheme and painted the main colors into the image. Save the image using the Iterative Save command. We are ready to start painting.

## Using Custom Brushes to Paint the Forest Background

Most of the work in this painting is development of a lush and wildly overgrown forest setting in which Red Riding Hood has been walking. We will use a number of techniques to create this cluttered and chaotic background. To paint the background, we will quickly use techniques in Painter that allow us to paint the impression of lots of detail without lots of effort: we will use a combination of custom paper textures, custom brushes, custom patterns, and custom image hose nozzles.

Perhaps you're wondering why we're putting so much work into creating custom assets. Surely if we spent the same amount of time just painting, we could accomplish just as much. Let me assure you that this is not case. A bit of time spent creating custom assets can save hours of work later on. An additional advantage is that the custom resources we create are reusable. Eventually, we will have a complete library of custom resources we've created that can be used in many ways and in many paintings, saving us hours of time in the future.

A portion of this tutorial will be showing how to create these custom assets and use them in a painting. In-depth instructions are available in the Painter manual and help file.

It would be way too difficult to try to get so specific that I tell you what brush to use and where. Because artists have their own way of working, individual and specific brushes will not be called for at every step. You should pick and use brushes you want when you want. Specifically, I mean that I will not specify using Leaf Brush number 1 or 2 or 3 at any specific or particular time. I will expect you to pick and choose your brushes, paper textures, and patterns and use them to create your own image.

We will be creating each type of asset step by step. We will not, however, be creating every brush, paper, or pattern used in the painting. All the different assets used to create this painting are available for you to download. In fact, there are more custom materials and libraries in the downloadable libraries than we used in the painting.

> **Note:** All the paper textures, patterns, brushes, and image hoses used in this tutorial are available for download at www.sybex.com/go/painter.

To begin, we will create a custom Leaf brush. This is an overview of the technique you could use to create your own brushes used in this painting; it is not a tutorial on all the features in Painter's Brush Creator.

The brush we will create is not the only one that is used to paint the background in the painting, but only one of many. All the brushes that we use in the painting are available for download at www.sybex.com/go/painter.

Let's create a Leaf brush that we can use to paint the background.

## Creating a Leaf Brush

The Leaf brush that we will create is one of many we will create using the same technique we'll use in the Red Riding Hood painting. The brush is created from a freeware dingbat font called Botarosa1. This font is freely available for download all over the Internet and is included with the downloads available to you with this book at www.sybex.com/go/painter. It is a simple font with some nice leaf shapes. Dingbat fonts are a great resource for creating custom brushes.

> **Note:** Install the Botarosa1 font before starting Painter.

The first thing to do when creating custom brush is to select an existing brush as the foundation of the new one. In this case, choose Dons brush as the base brush. This is a simple brush, just like the brush we will be creating. Try to pick basic brushes that have similar characteristics to the kind of brush you want to create.

To create a nice Leaf brush, do the following:

1. Create a new image that is approximately 600×600 pixels in size. The actual size of the image is really not critical.

   Make sure the paper color of this image is white. Brushes use only black-and-white information, and there's no reason to have a colored background.

2. Pick the Text tool, and click in your new image. From the Text Property Bar at the top of the screen, choose Botarosa1 from the drop-down list of available fonts.

3. Set Size to approximately 70 points using the Size slider, also in the Property Bar, just to the right of the Font drop-down list.

4. Click in your image and type **ABCDEF**. You should now see some nice leaf shapes, as in Figure 7.3.

   We can make each of these leaf shapes into a different brush. In this tutorial, we will use only the first shape.

Figure 7.3 Some nice leaf shapes are typed into the new image.

We need to convert the Text layer into a regular layer before we can continue.

5. Right-click on the Text layer and select Commit from the pop-up options. This changes the Text layer into a default layer.

6. Pick the Crop tool, and drag a selection around the first leaf. Move each edge of the crop box as close as possible to the leaf edges without intersecting them.

7. Crop the image so that only the first leaf remains.

8. Drop the Leaf layer onto the canvas.

9. Select the entire image.

10. In the Brush Selector bar, click the Palette menu arrow, and pick Capture Dab.

While it appears that nothing has happened, the selected image has actually been captured as a new brush dab. It might be possible to see a ghost image of the leaf around the brush cursor by moving the brush back over the image. Currently, the brush is not useful and needs some tweaking to make it behave so we can paint the leaves in our image.

### Tweaking the Custom Leaf Brush

To make these adjustments to the Leaf brush, we need to open the Brush Creator. There are two ways to access the Brush Creator; we can use the keyboard command Ctrl+B, or we can go to the window menu and choose Show Brush Creator.

The Brush Creator is a powerful tool that contains three different sections represented by tabs at the top of the window: Randomizer, Transposer, and Stroke Designer. We will concern ourselves only with the Stroke Designer.

I encourage you to learn to use the Brush Creator. You'll soon find that you will be creating custom brushes for almost every project you work on. In this case, we're going to use it to create just this one brush.

We can use this method to create additional brushes for this painting if we want to take the time.

The Brush Creator has several important areas. The large white area is called the Scratchpad, where we can test your brushstroke, and at the bottom of the window is the preview grid. The preview grid shows how our current stroke looks and automatically updates as we change any of the settings.

Go ahead and draw a stroke in the Scratchpad. The stroke does look somewhat like leaves, but the individual dabs are overlapping, and the leaf is pointed in only one direction. This is obviously not how you would want a Leaf brush to paint (Figure 7.4).

We will adjust some settings to make the Leaf brush behave more like we want.

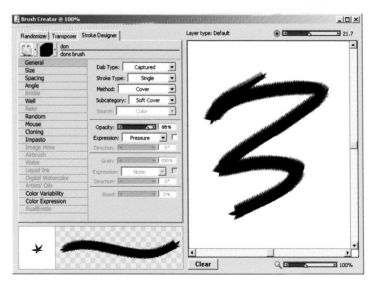

**Figure 7.4** The Brush Creator showing leaf dabs

We'll make these adjustments to the controls on the left side of the Brush Creator:

1. In the General controls, set the Opacity setting to 86%.

2. In the Size controls, set the Min Size slider to 85%. This lets the size of the dab vary between full size and 85% of full size. Then set the Expression drop-down menu to Random. This causes the size of each dab to be painted randomly.

3. In the Spacing controls, set the Spacing slider up to 200% and the Min spacing up to 20.

Go ahead and draw a stroke in the Scratchpad. Notice now, in the preview grid, there is quite a bit of space between each dab (Figure 7.5).

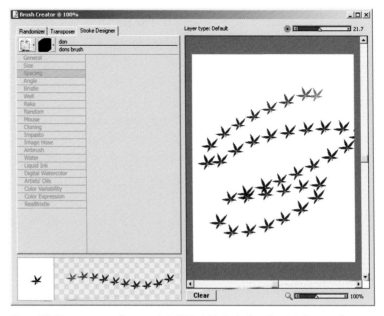

**Figure 7.5** You can see space between the individual dabs in the Scratchpad window now that spacing has been increased in the Spacing controls.

4. In the Angle controls, set the Squeeze slider up to 99% or less. You want a setting less than 100%. Choose Random from the Expression drop-down menu, and set the Angle Range to 360° and the Ang Step to anywhere between 1° and 5°.

Draw a new stroke in the Scratchpad, and notice how the leaves are painted randomly at different angles (Figure 7.6).

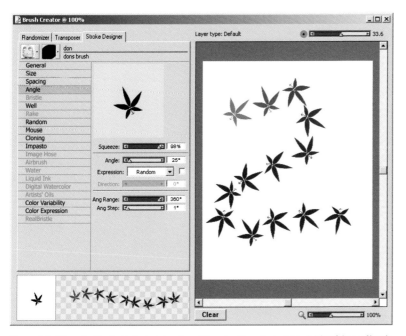

**Figure 7.6** After using the Angle Controls to set up different options, the individual dabs of the Leaf brush are now painted at random angles.

5. In the Random Controls, set the Jitter to 2.0. The Jitter randomly offsets the stroke in both the horizontal and vertical axes.

6. Use the Colors palette to choose a nice green color for the last adjustment to the brush. You will not notice any change if you leave the color set to black.

7. In the Color Variability controls, move the H slider to 5%, the S slider to 5%, and the V slider to 5%. These controls vary the color of each dab using that dab's Hue, Saturation, and Value settings.

To see the effect of these adjustments, we can fill the Scratchpad with strokes from our brush. The result is a slight variation in color of the individual leaves in the stroke (Figure 7.7).

8. In the Property Bar at the top of the screen, choose Variant and pick Save Variant. A box will pop up, and you can name your new brush.

When naming new brushes, it's important to give each a name that will adequately describe the brush. In this case, I simply named the brush `Leaf 01`.

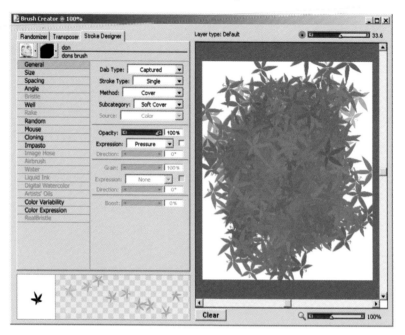

**Figure 7.7** With the Color Variability Controls adjusted, you can now see individual color variation in each dab of the Leaf brush.

### Restoring the Original Brush

One last thing that we want to do is restore the brush we began with to its original state. Unlike Photoshop, Painter remembers any changes we make to a brush and does not automatically default back to the original when we close the program. Because we made changes to the default Dons brush, it is now a Leaf brush and not the original Dons brush.

To restore the brush to its original state, we'll go to the Variant menu again and select Restore Default Variant. Dons brush is now restored to its original settings before we made any changes.

The newly created Leaf brush can be found in the same category as the original brush used to create it.

That is all there is to it. I used this technique to create each Leaf brush used in the painting. Now we will switch back to using these brushes and paint the background in the Red Riding Hood painting.

### Painting the Leafy Background

Now we have created a brush to use to paint the background. A number of additional brushes are available in the library that you have downloaded. If you've not yet installed those brushes, you might want to go ahead and do that because you will want to use more than one brush to paint the background. Forests have lots of different vegetation growing in them, and we want an organic feel, not a monotonous repetitive look in the background.

Once the brushes are installed, open the Red Riding Hood painting. Currently there are two layers in this file. There's the Canvas layer with the gradient and colors painted on it, and there's the Sketch layer above.

1. Create a new layer above the Canvas layer. Make sure the Pick Up Underlying Color box is checked.

2. Using various Leaf brushes, cover the background behind Red Riding Hood. Start with darker colors to look like deeper areas of the forest hidden in shadow, and work toward lighter colors in the front of the image. Don't worry if some of the leaves overlap into the character. You will either erase them or paint over them in later stages. Make sure that the size of the leaves varies from smaller in the background to larger in the foreground. You may also want to use the colors of the leaves to help set the character apart from the background (Figure 7.8).

3. Switch to the Variable Chalk brush. From the Papers palette, pick one of the stick paper textures and paint some stalks at the bottom edge of the leaves. Don't worry if the stick paper looks rather mechanical at this point. You'll fix that as you continue to paint.

**Figure 7.8** A layer of leaves has been painted above the Canvas layer and below the Sketch layer, beginning the initial work in the overgrown forest.

4. Continue to use the same brush, but switch the paper texture to Basic Paper, one of Painter's default papers, and paint the path that Red Riding Hood is standing on.

5. Choose the Eraser, and clean up any stray leaves or stick strokes that are covering Red Riding Hood.

6. Switch to the Sketch layer and, using the Eraser brush, clean up the sketch, getting rid of any of the messy strokes left from the original drawing.

7. Create a new layer above the leaves but below the sketch, choose Dons brush, and paint the colors of the character carefully on this new layer (Figure 7.9).

**Figure 7.9** The path that Red Riding Hood is walking on is painted using the Variable Chalk brush. The Eraser tool can clean up any stray leaf strokes that cover the figure. A new layer is created, and the colors in Red Riding Hood are carefully painted.

## Separating the Character and Background

I actually thought I would do most of the painting on one layer, but as I started to work, I could see that one layer would not do. It's necessary to separate the background from the character. The background needs more work than I originally thought, and trying to paint around the character would be tedious and difficult. The best thing would be to separate the background from the character; that way, I can work on the background without fear of overpainting the figure, and then work on the figure without fear of messing up my background.

It is easier to separate the background and character now, in the beginning stages of a painting, than to separate them later when more finished work is done.

Ideally, it would have been best to separate the character from the background while the painting was still just a sketch.

1. First, drop all the layers onto the canvas. Also, delete the extra Sketch layer since you're probably not going to need it again.

2. Because the colors in the image are quite distinct and separate, it is not too difficult to isolate the character. Select the background using the Magic Wand and the Rectangular Selection and Oval Selection tools.

3. With the majority of the background selected, invert the selection and use Save Selection in the Select menu.

4. Go into the Channels palette and paint on the Alpha layer to clean up the mask. When the Alpha layer is visible, it appears red at 50% opacity. You can paint on the Alpha layer using any brush.

Usually I use one of the Pen brushes that has a smooth edge and is very opaque. Using either black, which adds to the mask, or white, which erases from the mask, I clean up the edges and get rid of any stray areas outside or inside the mask.

5. If you have stray areas outside the figure in the background, you can use the Selection tools to select those areas and then use the Backspace key to clear them.

Figure 7.10 shows the mask created in the Alpha channel over the character.

6. It is a simple matter to load the selection based on the Alpha channel and either copy or cut Red Riding Hood out of the background and paste her into her own layer. When you have done this, make sure to save the image again using the Iterative Save feature.

**Figure 7.10** The mask is visible over the character.

## Painting the Separated Background

When Red Riding Hood is on her own layer, go back into the background and, using a variety of Leaf brushes, paint more and more foliage.

As you get closer to the path, switch from Leaf brushes to Stick brushes. The stick brushes were created in the same manner as the Leaf brushes. In fact, the ding-bat font used to create the leaves also has some characters that look like sticks. These characters were used to create the brushes.

 **Note:** The Stick brushes that I'm using can be found in this chapter's resources, which are available to download if you have not already done so at www.sybex.com/go/painter.

I don't want leaves going all the way to the ground; I would rather have some sticks and some grass growing up to meet the leaves. I paint sticks in dark greens knowing that, as I paint grass and more leaves, the sticks will recede into the shadows (Figure 7.11).

**Figure 7.11** Stick brushes are used to paint the lower edge of the foliage where it meets the path.

I don't want the forest to look completely friendly. I believe it can use a few more interesting shapes than just those created with the Leaf brushes. I decide I'm going to add a few thorn bushes.

Now, I could go ahead and paint these bushes by hand, but it would be rather tedious and could take a lot of time. Fortunately, Painter has a nice feature called Patterns that makes painting a series of thorny vines simple.

Most people's first thought when using Patterns in Painter is how to use them for backgrounds and textures. Actually, it was quite a while after I started using Painter that I discovered the true power of patterns. When we combine them with the Pattern Pen brushes, we have a whole new set of tools that can create some unique effects.

In this particular painting, we're going to use patterns to paint some thorny vines in our background forest.

Much of the time when I'm creating shapes that I will use in patterns, I do so in either Corel Draw or Adobe Illustrator. I could create the same shapes using Painter's Pen tool and will do so if it is a very simple shape. I just find it easier to do more complicated shapes in the other programs. There are also more options available in Draw and Illustrator, so most of the time I use these other programs.

I don't want to go into how to create shapes in Draw or Illustrator, so the file that I used is included in this chapter's assets. If you want to follow along and create your own thorns, you can use this or, if you would rather not bother creating a pattern right now, you can simply load the thorn pattern using the Pattern Mover and continue on to the next section.

> **Note:** The original file used to create a thorn pattern as well as the thorn pattern itself are available for download in this chapter's assets at www.sybex.com/go/painter.

To create a pattern to use with the pattern pens, do the following:

1. Open the file thorns.PSD (Figure 7.12).

**Figure 7.12** The thorns.psd file

This file consists of two layers: the Canvas layer and a Thorn layer. A Thorn layer consists of shapes created in Illustrator and exported as a Photoshop file. I do this using vector programs to get clean shapes. You can draw your shapes if you are not as concerned with accuracy. I often just draw them if I'm going to use the pattern in a rough painting. In this particular case, though, I wanted a very clean, precise, and relatively nasty-looking thorny vine.

For this thorn pattern, I want to use the transparency of the Thorn layer. To do this, I need to make sure that the Thorn layer is active before capturing my pattern. If the Canvas layer is active and I capture the pattern, I will not get the results I am hoping for.

2. With the Thorn layer active, choose Capture Pattern from the Palette menu. The Palette menu is accessed using the small palette menu triangle in the upper-right corner of the Patterns palette.

3. The Capture Patterns option box will open. Your preview should look something like Figure 7.13. Name the pattern, leave all the settings default, and click OK.

If your preview of the pattern looks like Figure 7.14, chances are the Canvas layer is the active layer. You could go ahead and save this pattern, but it will not behave correctly when you paint.

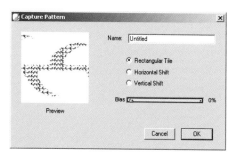

**Figure 7.13** The preview window of the Capture Pattern option box showing the pattern captured correctly

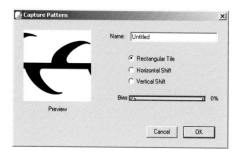

**Figure 7.14** The preview window of the Capture Pattern option box showing the pattern incorrectly captured

That's all there is to creating a pattern to paint thorny vines in our painting. In the next steps I will show you how to use the pattern we just created to add thorny vines to our painting.

## Painting Vines

1. Make sure that the Thorn pattern is the active pattern. If you cannot see thorns in the preview window, choose the Thorn pattern from the drop-down list.

2. In the Brush Selector, choose the Pattern Pen Masked. You can find this brush in the Pattern Pens category.

3. Create a new layer above the background and, using this brush, draw some long and graceful thorny vines. The vine pattern will follow the direction of your stroke (Figure 7.15).

**Figure 7.15** Long, graceful, thorny vines are drawn on a new layer using the Pattern Pen Masked and the thorn pattern we just created.

The potential creativity using this brush is limited only by your imagination. You can use it to draw almost anything, from chains, tree branches, and trunks to jungle vines and jewelry—virtually anything that you need to paint in a long and continuous path, and even some things that don't need to be in a path.

Though the thorns are drawn, they are a little rough, and the black is a little too stark for the painting. To make them integrate into the background better, follow these steps:

1. Check the Preserve Transparency box with the Thorn layer active.

2. Using Dons brush, paint some dark olive green colors over the thorns. Because the Preserve Transparency box is checked, you don't need to worry about painting outside the thorns. A few large strokes, and you'll be done.

3. Apply the Soften effect to the thorns. Use the default settings and click OK.

4. Uncheck the Preserve Transparency box and use the Soften effect once again. This time lower the amount to something between 2 and 2.5.

5. Lower the Thorn layer Opacity setting to 85%.

The thorns are finished. They add some graceful curves to the background forest and improve the overall composition of the painting (Figure 7.16).

Create another layer over the thorny vines, and paint a few more leaves. Drop the Leaf and Vine layers onto the canvas (Figure 7.17).

**Figure 7.16** A Thorn layer is painted using the Pattern brush, and a few small adjustments are made to the layer so it integrates into the background.

**Figure 7.17** A new layer is created, and additional leaves are painted over the Vine layer.

The background is looking pretty good. The transition area between the background foliage and the path is pretty sparse. We need to paint some grass over this area to give it detail.

In the next section, we will make a grass paper texture and use it to paint grass in the path.

## Making a Grass Paper Texture

Using simple image-based paper textures is one of the best ways to paint repetitive elements in any painting. Paper textures are easy to use, and they don't take much time to make. In this section, I will show you how to make a simple paper texture that looks like grass. We will use the new texture to add grass to the transition area between the foliage and the path in our painting.

If you do not want to create a paper texture at this time, you can use the assets that are available to download. Both the paper texture and the image file used to create the texture are available to download at www.sybex.com/go/painter.

> **Note:** The paper texture library and original file used to create one of the grass paper textures are available for download at www.sybex.com/go/painter.

To create a new paper texture that looks like grass, follow these steps:

1. Create a new image that is 700 pixels wide by 200 pixels tall. The exact dimensions of the image are not that important, but something around this size will work well.
2. Choose the Flat Color brush from the Pens category.
3. Using black as your color, draw a number of grass-like strokes across the image.

Do not worry about trying to draw strokes that look exactly like blades of grass. It should take you no more than a minute or two to draw all the strokes. You will have an image that looks something like Figure 7.18.

Figure 7.18  A number of quickly drawn strokes that will be used to create a grassy paper texture

4. Select the entire image.
5. From the Papers palette menu, choose Capture Paper.

6. The Save Paper box appears. Name your new paper, and set the Crossfade slider to 0. Click OK.

7. The preview window in the Papers palette will update and show your new paper texture as the active paper.

That is the basic method used to create a paper texture in Painter. You can quickly and easily create a library of paper textures to use in any project.

Consult the Painter help file to learn how to save individual libraries using the Paper Mover.

Now that we have created a grass paper texture, let's check out how the texture will work in a test image.

1. Create a new image that is about 900×900 pixels.

2. Pick the Variable Chalk brush.

3. Choose a nice green color from the Colors palette.

4. Draw some grass in your image.

Your image probably looks something like Figure 7.19. It is likely that this is not what you expected to see, and it would not be very useful in the painting process. The result is way too mechanical and not nearly random enough to paint convincing grass.

**Figure 7.19** The results of painting with the newly created paper texture. The results are not what we want.

There is not actually a problem with the paper texture. It will work just fine if we make one more adjustment. Interestingly enough, it is an adjustment to the brush we will be painting with.

5. From the Window menu, select Brush Controls Show Random. The Brush Controls appear with the Random controls expanded. Check the Random Brush Stroke Grain box.

6. Now go back to the image and paint once again using the Variable Chalk brush.

Checking the box causes Painter to randomly move the paper texture as each dab is painted. The overall effect is very random and appears much more organic, as you can see in Figure 7.20.

**Figure 7.20** Checking the Random Brush Stroke Grain box causes Painter to randomly move the paper texture as you paint, giving a much more organic result.

Remember though, that this is a change to the brush and not the paper texture. Painter will remember this change each time you use this brush unless you tell it to restore the default variant.

**Note:** There are several premade grass paper textures in the library.

7. Now go back to the painting and create a new layer above the Canvas layer.

8. Use the Variable Chalk brush that has the Random Brush Stroke Grain box checked and paint a layer of grassy strokes blending the path into the foliage.

You can switch between paper textures as you paint, so vary the paper textures you use to give a more natural-appearing grassy edge. There is even a clover paper texture in the library for you to try.

10. When you're happy with the look of your grassy edge, drop the layer onto the canvas.

Your image should now look something like Figure 7.21.

**Figure 7.21** A grassy edge transitioning from the path to the leafy undergrowth has been painted using custom paper textures.

The final step in painting the background will be to use a custom image hose nozzle and paint a number of hand-painted blades of grass at the front edge of the background.

## Building a Grass Nozzle File

Using hand-painted grass will help unify the figure with the background. Up to this point, there has been a lot of detail in the background, but because none of it has been hand-painted, it has a different style than Red Riding Hood.

As with earlier sections in this chapter, you have the option of building a nozzle or simply using one of the assets provided. The nozzle files used in the painting are available for download at www.sybex.com/go/painter. One version includes drop shadows and the second just the blades of grass.

If you are going to use the downloaded nozzle files, you can skip this section and go on to the next.

**Note:** The nozzle files used in the tutorial are available for download at www.sybex.com/go/painter.

The first step to building a grass nozzle file to use with the Image Hose is to paint a number of individual blades of grass.

1. Create a new file that is approximately 1200 pixels wide by 300 pixels high.

2. Create a new layer.

3. Paint 8 or 10 individual blades of grass using Dons brush or any other brush you would like to use. Paint all the blades of grass on the transparent layer (Figure 7.22). Your blades of grass will probably look quite a bit different from mine, but that's just fine.

**Figure 7.22** Blades of grass created for the nozzle files.

4. Select each blade of grass, and cut and paste it into a new layer. It is important that each blade of grass is on its own layer.

5. Select all the layers by holding down the Shift key and clicking on each layer in the Layer palette, using the keyboard combination Ctrl+Shift+1, or using the Layers palette menu and choosing Select All Layers.

6. Group all the selected layers using the keyboard combination Ctrl+G.

7. From the Nozzle palette, choose Make Nozzle from Group.

A new RIF file is created and displayed on the screen. The individual blades of grass have been arranged in a grid on a black background. You will not be able to see the grid, but each cell is as large as needed to encompass the largest single element.

8. Save the file in Painter's native RIF format, adding a suffix nozzle to the filename.

It is always a good idea to add the word nozzle as a suffix to the file; otherwise, you will have difficulty trying to decide which files are nozzles and which are regular files. It gets harder as you make more custom nozzles.

That's all there is to making a simple nozzle file. Of course, the more images you begin with, the less repetition the nozzle file will have. Quite often I simply take the entire layer of objects, make a duplicate layer, and flip that layer horizontally, instantly doubling the number of individual elements in the nozzle.

We will use this file to paint some grass in our painting.

When we use the image hose, painting grass is a pretty straightforward process. Normally, it wouldn't merit its own short section, but there is one trick I want to show you that will make the grass look a lot better.

1. Choose the Image Hose brush, Dons Foliage spray. This brush is simply a default image hose with a couple of adjustments made so it will paint the nozzle in a predictable way.

2. Click the secondary color square in the Colors palette, and then choose a dark green color from within the painting using the eyedropper.

We'll go ahead and click the primary color once we've picked a dark green secondary color. We want to do this so that when we go back to regular painting and use the eyedropper to choose colors, we're not choosing colors for the secondary color. Most brushes paint with the primary color, and if we're choosing secondary colors instead, painting can become a very frustrating experience.

3. In the options bar, lower the Grain slider to about 40%.

By using the Grain slider, we can influence how much of the secondary color is mixed with the image hose nozzle. This is a great way to make one image hose paint multiple areas. For example, we might want to paint a row of leaves that appears to be in shadow, so we would lower the percentage of grain using the slider. We can use the same image hose to paint leaves in sunlight by raising the grain amount to 100%. At 100%, we are using the image hose with the original colors just as you created it.

4. Paint a row or two of grass across the bottom of the image (Figure 7.23).

**Figure 7.23** A darker line of grass painted using the image hose brush with the grain slider set to 40%

5. Now raise the Grain to 100% and paint another row of brighter grass across the darker grass (Figure 7.24).

6. Go ahead and continue to paint as much grass as you want in the background. This grass adds more detail and helps visually integrate Red Riding Hood into the background.

The background is now complete. All that we need to do now is to finish painting Red Riding Hood and her gun.

**Figure 7.24** Another line of grass is painted with the grain slider set to 100%.

## Painting Red Riding Hood

Painting Red Riding Hood is a straightforward process. Virtually all of the painting was done using Dons brush. There are not many tricks and techniques in this section. You should go about painting the character any way you would like her to appear. If you're not quite sure what to do, use my image as reference.

We paint Red Riding Hood on her own layer and use the Eraser to clean up any stray edges. The gun is completely made up. Use your creativity and do whatever you would like with its design. Maybe you want to make it into a light saber? Anyway, let your imagination run free.

There can be some difficulty when painting this much red into a green background. Use the whites in both the gun and Red Riding Hood's dress to help unify the color scheme by making the whites more blue-green than gray. I also made the fabric in Red Riding Hood's basket quite green to help tie the figure into the background. Also notice that some brown colors in the basket are similar to the browns used in the thorny vines. All of these small touches help create a painting with a harmonious color scheme. You do not want any one area isolated.

## Adding Weave to the Basket

The pattern on the fabric in the picnic basket is one from the Weaves palette.

1. Create a new layer.

2. Select the area over the picnic basket using the Rectangular Selection tool.

3. Fill the selected area with a weave.

4. Change the Composite Method of the layer to Overlay.

5. Erase everything outside of the edges of the fabric.

6. Lower the Opacity setting of the layer to about 60%.

7. Use the Soften effect at the default settings to slightly blur the weave pattern (Figure 7.25).

**Figure 7.25** Red Riding Hood, her pistol, and the picnic basket are all painted using Dons brush. A weave pattern has been added over the picnic basket fabric.

The painting is 99 percent finished at this point. We just need to add a few finishing touches, and we will be done.

# Finishing Touches

I want to add a little bit more detail and finish to the path. Right now, the bottoms of the blades of grass are floating just a little bit. If I paint up some dark gravel around them, it should help make them look like they are anchored to the ground.

I am going to use a custom brush called Gravel Painter to add some dirt around the bases of the grass. This brush is located in the brush library downloaded for the book at www.sybex.com/go/painter.

> **Note:** The Gravel Painter brush is available for download, as are all the other brushes used in these tutorials at www.sybex.com/go/painter.

## Anchoring with Gravel and Shadow

We are going to paint the gravel on a new layer created above the canvas but underneath Red Riding Hood.

1. Create a new layer above the canvas but below Red Riding Hood.
2. Pick the Gravel brush and, starting with a darker brown, paint under the blades of grass, gradually getting lighter toward the bottom of the painting.
3. Paint the shadow under Red Riding Hood with the same dark brown colors used under the grass.
4. When the path is painted to your satisfaction, go ahead and drop the layer onto the canvas.

That's all there is to finishing up the path. Custom brushes can make such chores go very quickly and easily.

## Adding Texture to Red's Cape

For a final touch, we will add some pattern to Red Riding Hood's cape. To do this, I will use a different paper texture and the good old Variable Chalk brush.

1. Create a new layer.
2. Choose one of the Wallpaper paper textures. These textures are also available for download if you have not already done so at www.sybex.com/go/painter.
3. Using the Variable Chalk brush and a red color selected from the lighter areas of Red Riding Hood's cape, lightly paint texture over the cape.
4. Erase any of the brushstrokes that overlap into the background.
5. Duplicate the layer.
6. Hide the bottom layer so only the top pattern layer is visible.
7. Lower the Opacity setting of the layer until the light pattern is just visible in the light areas of the cape.

8. Using the Eraser, erase any of the pattern that is in shadow areas.

9. Reveal the hidden layer and change its Composite Method to Multiply.

10. Lower the Opacity setting of the Multiply layer until it is just visible in the darker and shadowy areas of the cape.

11. Erase any of the dark patterns that overlap into the light areas of the cape.

12. When the patterns look good over the cape, select both layers and Red Riding Hood's layer and collapse them together.

13. Use the Eraser to clean up any edges that may have gotten messy when collapsing the layers.

Red Riding Hood is finished (Figure 7.26).

**Figure 7.26** Red Riding Hood's cape is finished.

## A Little Lighting

The painting is finished, but the lighting effects often give that little extra sparkle to a painting. The final touch I use is to add a lighting effect over the whole image.

So in this painting, as in earlier paintings, I add a lighting effect from the Effects > Surface Control > Apply lighting menu. At this point, you should choose any of the effects you like. I again use the Splashy Color preset.

The effect was too intense, so using Fade from the Edit menu, I reduced the effect 50%.

Now the painting is finally and completely finished (Figure 7.27).

**Figure 7.27** A lighting effect is added to finish the painting.

## Final Thoughts

It seems like we've covered just about every possible subject in Painter, though in reality we covered only a few. It is important to see how you can build a complicated and detailed background using just a few of the more normal features among all the available ones. We really only used paper textures, patterns, and the image hose to create a very thick and dense forest undergrowth.

I do hope that you will find these techniques useful in your own personal projects. Don't worry if it takes a little bit of practice before you are comfortable using them all together. Ultimately, you will have a great arsenal of techniques to use when you work with digital paint.

# From Concept to Complete

*A lot of work that I do is designing characters, creatures, environments, buildings, and other elements that may be needed in a video game, film, television work, or book covers.*

*The subject of this chapter is based on a project where I designed a number of different creatures to represent an imaginary monster with some health issues. This creature is a variation of one of the original sketches. It is more like monster design, the sequel.*

*In this chapter, we will paint the creature using some of the most typical methods I've used when doing this kind of work. This is not the most technical chapter in the book, but it may be the most useful because of its simplicity and straightforward approach.*

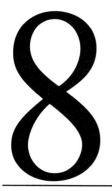

**Chapter Contents**

## Defining Concept Work

When I am speaking about concept work, usually I am talking about coming up with ideas for a client based on what they need to accomplish as opposed to drawing or painting my own ideas.

A lot of concept work never gets beyond the initial pencil sketch. Often the client can tell from a simple pencil sketch whether an idea is on track. Occasionally, though, additional work is needed to bring the idea to life. Usually it is a matter of doing more work on the original sketch. Often the work is nothing more than adding some value to give the sketch a more solid feel. Every so often, though, the ideal scenario happens, and I get to paint the original concept in color. Usually I use just one of the original sketches as the basis and integrate any additional ideas or refinements suggested by the client.

The concept for the creature in this chapter never went beyond the original pencil sketch stage and was not one of the designs chosen for the project. Most of my rejected ideas simply end up in the trash can. Often I like the original sketches that were not chosen just as much as the sketches that were used. In this case, I liked most of the original sketches more than the one that was ultimately chosen. That's why I decided to paint the beast for my own enjoyment and for this chapter.

The techniques used in this chapter are not particularly complicated. I use them because they are quick. Some of the painting uses techniques that I've described in detail in earlier chapters. I won't repeat them in great depth.

## Setting Up the Image

As with other images in the book, to set up the image, I scan the sketch at 300 dpi (dots per inch), though I usually find that the full-sized scan is too big to paint comfortably. So once I've opened the sketch, I generally reduce its size using the Canvas menu commands and selecting Resize. You can also use the keyboard combination Shift+Ctrl+R on the PC or Shift+Command+R if you're working on a Mac. I am most comfortable working on an image that is about 2000 pixels in its greatest dimension. The size of this sketch is reduced to around 1600 pixels wide and about 100 pixels tall. This is an easy size image to work with.

I will gradually increase the image size to whatever dimensions I need for the final printed version. This way I can paint the initial image quickly without worrying about painting in too much detail.

As I gradually increase the size, I will concentrate my painting efforts in the areas where there is the greatest detail. Larger areas like the background will not suffer or get too soft as the size of the image increases.

You have heard me say in this and other chapters that I scan the sketch at 300 dpi but I think that's too large to comfortably paint on. You may be asking why I don't just scan the sketch at the size I want for the painting. The short answer is that I never know when I might want to print the original sketch at full size, so it's best to have a scan that I can use for that purpose without any loss of quality. Most of the time, the final paintings done from sketches are the same size if not larger than the original sketches.

Figure 8.1 shows the sketch that I'm going to use for this painting. You will notice that it is not strictly a black-and-white sketch. This is not due to the scanning process or any postproduction adjustments but is actually how the sketch looked. It was drawn on slightly textured paper with a black grape Prismacolor pencil. Black grape is one of my favorite pencil colors. It is a nice dusty and dark violet color.

**Figure 8.1** Original creature sketch

Unlike the examples used in other chapters where the sketch is scanned in color but then the saturation is lowered until the drawing is just black and white, here I am going to leave the colors intact. The color of the scanned sketch fits with the color scheme I anticipate using.

When the paper that I sketch on has a texture like this one does, I try to let it show in the final image. Most of the time the paper texture gets covered up anyway.

The only real adjustment I make to the sketch is a slight increase in contrast using the Brightness/Contrast effect found under the Effects > Tonal Control menu.

**Note:** The sketch is available for download if you would like to follow along at www.sybex .com/go/painter, or you could use any of your own drawings.

## Setting the Mood and Tone

I try very early to set the mood and tone of a painting. Often I do several small thumbnails to try various color schemes. The advantage of this approach is that once you start painting on the final image, you're not making choices off the top of your head. This approach makes it possible to avoid a lot of mistakes later on.

The best way to quickly make a number of color studies is to make a small duplicate of the sketch and then quickly paint color over it. I'm not worried at all about any detail; I'm simply trying to establish value patterns in a color scheme. If I'm concerned about the mood of an image, this is the best time to consider that. In this case, I know that I want a darker and more ominous and creepy feeling, so I limit my colors to darker hues.

### Playing with Color Schemes

Once I have done one small color study, I make six or eight duplicate layers and then, using Adjust Colors from the Effects menu, I move the Saturation slider and the Hue Shift slider to get variations on the original theme. I then go back on each of these different colored layers and paint in any additional colors I think they might need. I find this a quick and easy way to play with multiple color schemes and make sure I get the one that best suits my needs (Figure 8.2).

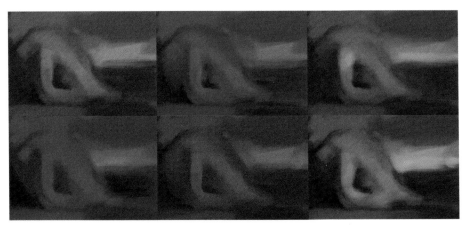

**Figure 8.2** Several small color studies done in preparation for the final painting

After having made several of the small color thumbnails, I decide on a rather golden yet very dark color scheme. I will accent the golden colors with some violets and reds. I want this image to have a rather heavy and oppressive atmosphere to it. The monster himself looks rather oppressed, and he is definitely heavy. He is rather like a large gooey cross between an octopus and a banana slug. In fact, the juxtaposition of these two animals is one of the determining factors in the choice of the color scheme. There is the yellow banana slug mixed with the multiple colors you can find on an octopus.

While all this talk of color scheme choice and what creatures influence the design of the creature does not directly show in the painting, it is important to know the reasoning behind an image, and it's important for you to know why I do things the way I do.

I begin adding color to this painting in a slightly different method than in some of the other chapters. I create a new layer and begin painting darker colors on it using Dons Digital Water 2 brush. This brush immediately changes the Composite Method of the layer to Gel. Gel and Multiply are perfect Composite Methods to use when establishing initial color schemes. The nice thing is that since this brush changes the layer immediately on its own, I don't have to think about it and can concentrate on the colors I want to use.

**Note:** Dons Digital Water 2 brush is one in the library of brushes available for download at www.sybex.com/go/painter.

I use a wide range of gold and slightly green colors to cover the whole surface of the painting. I put in some reds around the base of the beast and some subtle violet colors around his eyes. I make no effort to try to paint in any detail at this point because all I'm trying to do is establish the color and generally how dark I want the painting to appear.

The Digital Watercolor brush is a good brush to use because it blends nicely with the colors already painted, and you can make any corrections or changes in the colors used simply by painting with the new color. A similar approach would be to paint on a layer with the Composite Method set to Color; however, the effect is not nearly as dramatic, and the colors don't blend quite as nicely.

## Choosing the Light Source

I also decide where my main light source will be shining from. In this painting, it will be from the top right, slightly in front of the character. It is important to decide as early as possible what direction light will be coming from in any painting so you maintain a consistent lighting scheme throughout the painting.

Figure 8.3 shows the golden colors painted on the new Gel layer using a Digital Watercolor brush. The color scheme and mood of the painting is basically set at this point.

So you can see exactly how little detail is painted in this initial color lay-in, Figure 8.4 shows the painting with only the Color layer visible and the Sketch layer hidden. As you can see, the strokes are rough, made with a large brush and with virtually no attention given to any detail. You can also see that, while the majority of the colors are brown to golden, there are quite a large number of complementary violet colors interspersed throughout the image.

**Figure 8.3** The color scheme and values of the painting are set early using a Digital Watercolor brush.

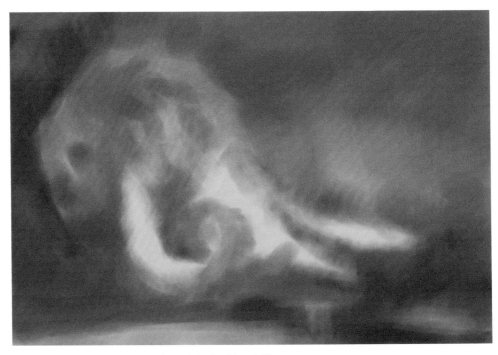

**Figure 8.4** The colors in the painting visible with the Sketch layer hidden

I want to darken the image even more. There are several ways I can do this:

- I can duplicate the original Gel layer.

- I can use the total controls in the Effects menu to adjust the brightness and contrast.

- I can use a lighting effect.

- I can create a new layer and use the Digital Watercolor brush once again to paint another Gel layer over the first.

- I can use a combination of all the above.

In this case, I choose to create a new layer and again, using the Digital Watercolor brush, paint additional colors over the whole image. This approach gives me the greatest flexibility with my choices of color, and changes are easy should I want to go back later.

I create a new layer and, using Dons Digital Watercolor 2 brush, paint a completely new colored layer. On this layer, I use more violet and gray colors than on the first layer (Figure 8.5). Notice that there is even less attention to detail on this new layer. A large brush is used with quick strokes.

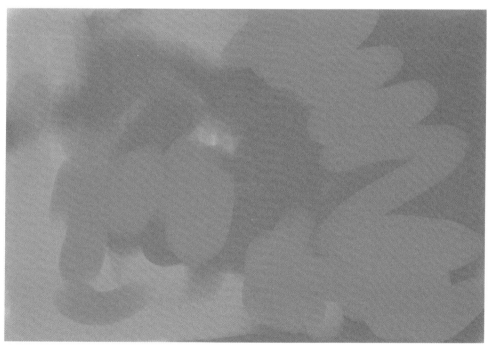

**Figure 8.5** A new layer is created and more color is painted on the image using Dons Digital Watercolor 2 brush. The figure shows the new layer isolated from the rest of the painting so the individual colors can be seen.

The whole image is now way too dark, so the Opacity setting of the last layer is lowered to 33% (Figure 8.6).

The mood and tone of the painting are set. The painting has a rather heavy and oppressive atmosphere, which is what I was after. The piece would not have been nearly as effective if it were painted a nice blue/pink color scheme.

**Figure 8.6** The painting with the new layer visible. Its Opacity setting has been lowered to 33% so the painting is not too dark.

## Painting the Monster

Now that the color and mood of the painting are set, it's time to start painting the creature.

We will use a simple approach to paint this monster. The idea when doing concept art is to get the job done well and as quickly as possible. To these ends, we won't use a lot of special effects in this painting. We will use a few paper textures to give some texture to the monster's skin, but for the most part we will use only a few brushes to complete the whole painting. At the completion of the painting, we will try a few shortcuts described in earlier chapters to add a reflection of the monster in the foreground.

As you follow along, please realize that this is just one of many approaches I will use when painting. There are many other ways you can accomplish the same task. Following along with my example will show you how I go about painting an image when I need to get the job done quickly. Experiment as you paint. You may find a technique that works better for you and is quicker than the way I do things.

### Making More Monster

First I want to make a little more monster. I think he could use another large tentacle on the far side of his body. Of course, it really doesn't matter; I can add as many or as few additional features as I would like. Part of the fun of doing this kind of work is letting the image grow. I would not, however, start adding parts and pieces to this painting if I were actually painting it for a client. Most of the time, the client simply wants to see the original idea with any already-agreed-upon changes painted.

But for now, let's go ahead and add in a new tentacle.

1. Add a new layer on top of the Canvas layer.

2. Select one of the Pencil brushes. It really doesn't matter which brush you choose at this point since all we are going to be doing is sketching.

3. Draw a new tentacle on the new layer.

Don't try to add any more detail than is in the sketch at this point. You want to keep the drawing open to adjustments and changes. Adding more detail early on only makes it more difficult should you need to make changes. For some reason, the more time we spend on a drawing or painting, the more it gets progressively harder to go back and alter what is already done.

As you can see in my painting, the new tentacle is really little more than a scribble at this point. I have also added a number of ribbon-like extensions or fins coming from the monster's back. I've drawn just enough to give me direction as I continue but not so much that I will hesitate to make alterations (Figure 8.7).

**Figure 8.7** A new tentacle has been added to the monster on a new layer using one of the pencils.

I go back and select the most basic brush that I use: Dons brush. It's a simple brush that allows me to quickly paint a lot of color in varying opacities.

4. Create a new layer on top of all the layers.

5. Using Dons brush and selecting the colors from within the image, begin to add form to the monster.

Whenever possible, I choose colors from within the image. Not only does this speed up the actual painting, but it helps maintain color harmony.

To keep my forms solid and three-dimensional (3D) looking, I paint my strokes across the large excess of each form. For example, most of this monster is rather long and horizontal, so instead of making large strokes of color in a horizontal direction, I make shorter strokes of color in a more vertical direction.

Usually when I'm painting, I work from the darker colors to the lighter ones. In this case, where most of the painting is already quite dark, I start by adding some lighter color. Because the painting is relatively dark, I can easily decide just how light I want to take these colors, whereas in a normal painting, it is often hard to see light color until a lot of the darks are established (Figure 8.8).

**Figure 8.8** A new layer has been created on top of all the other layers, and some lighter colors are painted onto this layer using Dons brush.

The painting progresses quite quickly at this point.

**6.** Paint the rear tentacle and add some big blister-like features on the monster's back.

**7.** Paint some slightly brighter red color into the suckers on the tentacles (Figure 8.9). It's a good idea when painting to keep your brightest colors in the areas of greatest interest or where you want the viewer to look.

Also, notice how I am keeping my strokes as a vertical block in the larger shapes, which gives a sense of 3D form to the shapes. I'm not concerned about covering the sketch. I figure that the whole thing is an idea in progress, and I don't want to get locked into filling in the lines.

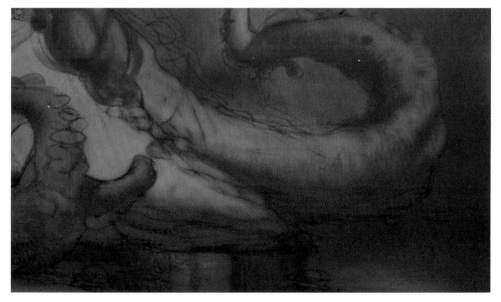

**Figure 8.9** Slightly brighter red colors painted into the suckers on the tentacles

Now we switch between two brushes to do most of the painting. I use a combination of Dons brush and the default Opaque Round brush, found in the Oils category of brushes.

The Opaque Round brush is one of my favorites. It paints with a number of small bristle-like strokes. You can adjust the number of bristles using the Feature slider in the options bar. Lower numbers give you solid strokes with many bristles, and higher values give sparse strokes with just a few bristles (Figure 8.10).

Feature settings

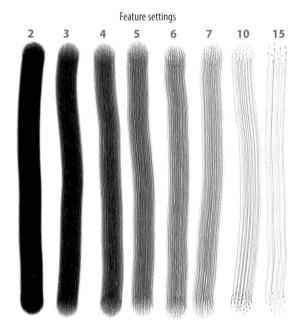

**Figure 8.10** Different values in the Feature option give you thick or sparse Opaque Round brushstrokes.

The early stages of painting the face have begun. Switch between the Opaque Round and Dons brush as you work on the face.

1. In the eye areas, paint violet colors that are complementary to the overall color scheme.

2. Paint some rich and dark reds into the nose and mouth areas.

While these areas are important to the overall look of the painting, I want them to appear a bit mysterious, so I keep most of the colors quite dark (Figure 8.11).

**Figure 8.11** The face of the monster is starting to take shape.

I also keep the face dark and slightly obscure because the viewer's imagination is much more powerful than my brush when filling in the details. This is not to say you should leave everything vague, as there is some danger of the painting not looking finished, but you can leave some of it up to the viewer's imagination.

I am pretty happy with how the painting is progressing. The monster is starting to look pretty creepy, the values of the painting are working well, and there's a nice color harmony to the whole image.

I want to reestablish the drawing. As we've been painting, we've covered the original sketch. This really doesn't matter because we've added enough new material that the original sketch does not include everything we are currently painting. I want to draw the far tentacle and the ribbon-like extensions on the monster's back with a better idea of where I want to take them as they are painted.

3. Using Dons brush and a small size, redraw the far tentacle in the ribbon-like appendages on the monster's back (Figure 8.12).

**Figure 8.12** Using Dons brush, the back and far tentacle of the monster are drawn in more detail.

### Developing a Wet and Gooey Look

I envisioned this monster from the beginning to be a wet, gooey kind of creature. Right now he's neither wet nor gooey. We will add most of the highlights at the end of the painting, but we want to start developing that wet shiny look early on to make sure it's going to work.

### Adding a Little Shine

One of the easiest ways to add some shine to anything you paint is to add some bright highlights. An easy way to paint these highlights is with a default Painter brush, the Glow brush. This brush is found in the FX category.

The Glow brush is another of my favorite brushes. You need to be careful when using this brush, though, as the effect it paints can be quickly overdone.

1. Choose the Glow brush, and in the options bar, set the Strength to 8% and the Grain to 8%. Lowering these settings makes the stroke easier to control.

2. Choose a nice bright color from the Colors palette. The brush will use this color to produce a glowing effect. You'll want to pick a color that is similar to the area you'll be painting. In this particular example, I select a bright gold color.

3. Using a small brush size and light touch on the stylus, paint some glowing strokes on the monster.

Don't make your highlights too large. The larger the beast, the smaller you'll want to paint the individual highlights. This assumes that the creature's hide is not perfectly smooth and is made up of a number of smaller scales, or bumps, or something similar. Figure 8.13 shows the initial experiment at creating highlights on the monster's hide.

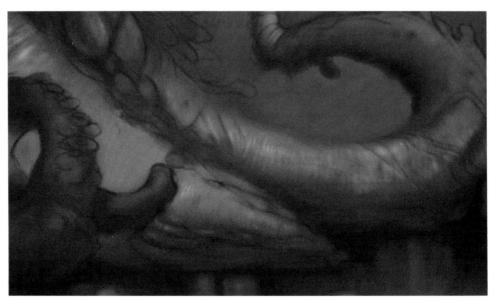

**Figure 8.13** Some highlights have been added to the monster using the Glow brush.

While I have not specifically stated that you should be saving your image, you should be. Especially make sure that you save the image before and after any major change. It is assumed from this point on that you will save consistently. I won't mention it again.

### Working with Color Layers

I want to vary the color on the monster's back where the big blister-like features are painted. The easiest way to do this is using the Color layer. A Color layer is a convenient way to either add or change color in any painting. Of course, one of the main advantages is that you are not committed to that change and can easily modify the colors any time. In fact, it is easy to use a Color layer and do away with color entirely. If you want to eliminate the colors in your image, you can simply paint with gray on a Color layer.

1. Create a new layer.
2. Change the Composite Method of the new layer to Color.
3. Using the Digital airbrush, paint some orange color over the blister area of the monster.
4. Use the Soften effect to get rid of any artifacts or strange edges the airbrush may leave.
5. Adjust the intensity of the new color by lowering or increasing the Opacity setting of the layer.

Figure 8.14 shows how easy it is using a Color layer to adjust the hue of any section in a painting. In this case, the Color layer has been used to change the colors on the back of the monster.

**Figure 8.14**  A Color layer has been used to change the back of the monster from gold to a more orange hue.

### Giving the Monster Texture

The painting is coming along nicely, and the monster's colors are working well. We want to go ahead and add more detail to the beast using the same techniques described in earlier chapters. The creative use of paper textures can not only add detail but add that detail quickly and easily.

The textures in this painting are located in a paper library called Hides and Skin. If you've not already done so, you should download this paper library now.

> **Note:** The paper library Hides and Skin is available for download www.sybex.com/go/painter.

None of the brushes we've been painting with up to this point interact with any paper texture, so we need to choose a different brush that does. Go ahead and use the brush we have used so many times before when we've wanted to paint texture: the Variable Chalk brush. If you don't remember, this is a default Painter brush that can be found in the Chalk category.

1.  Load or append the Hides and Skin paper library.
2.  Choose the Variable Chalk brush.

3. Create a new layer on which to paint some of the monster's hide.

4. Pick a darker color from an area already painted on the monster and paint some bumpy, hide-like patterns there.

5. Create another layer on which to paint some lighter bumps on top of those already painted.

6. Pick a lighter color from somewhere on the monster.

7. Invert the paper texture.

8. Paint some lighter spots into the darker hide you just painted.

9. Using the Soften effect, slightly blur both the light and dark layers.

10. Use the Eraser tool to clean up any strokes that strayed into the background or onto adjacent areas of the monster where you don't want texture.

11. Use the Eraser tool and paint on the edges of the texture to fade them into the surrounding areas.

12. Vary the Opacity setting of the light and dark layers to make the effect subtle yet still obvious.

Figure 8.15 shows some texture painted onto the monster to give more interest and credibility to the skin.

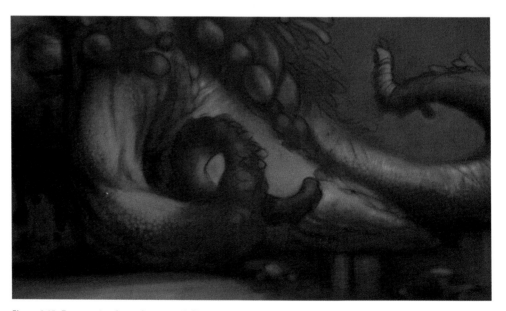

**Figure 8.15** Texture painted onto the monster's skin.

When painting texture into any creature, you do not want even coverage over the whole beast. Any texture that covers too evenly looks artificial. The goal of using these textures is to add an additional impression of realism to the painting. Also remember to vary the size of the skin textures. Larger textures can be used in larger areas of the body, while smaller textures should be used in areas such as the face, the hands, or anywhere that there is more detail.

The paper library includes a number of different textures. There are no right or wrong textures to use. Any of them will work, and you should pick one or several that look good to you.

**13.** When the skin textures are finished to your satisfaction, drop all the layers onto the canvas.

Because the background is going to be left much as it already appears, there's no reason to paint the monster on a separate layer. Dropping the layers makes it easier to lose some of the monster's edges into the background colors, helping build the final mood of the painting.

## Finishing the Monster

The monster is coming along quite well at this point. We added some textures to give the skin a more realistic appearance, we have some nice highlights, the colors are harmonious and working well together, and the values work. We are satisfied with the monster so far, so we will use the same techniques to continue painting.

We will concentrate on adding a few more details to the monster himself as well as start to paint some of the background.

We'll do most of the work on the creature on the Canvas layer. Painting on the Canvas layer is much quicker than constantly moving between different layers. When we need a layer to make a task easier, we will, of course, create a new layer and use it. Using a limited number of brushes also helps speed up the painting process. We will be using only the three brushes that have been used for the majority of the painting. Those brushes are Dons brush, Opaque Round, and Glow brush.

Much of the painting on the monster from this point on is really up to the individual artist's vision and taste. Artists have their own style and areas that they want to draw attention to. Because of this, I will list only the areas where I did additional work and then show you the painting. Follow along as much or as little as you would like.

### Refining the Monster Details

Figure 8.16 shows a lot of additional work done on the monster as well as a bit of work done in the foreground area. I gave the following areas the most attention.

- I refined the features in the face. I added some creases and folds around the eyes, nose, and mouth.
- I added a lot of small teeth to the mouth. When painting teeth, don't paint them too white. There is a general tendency to paint teeth too light and too white. We all want a white smile, but it is not necessary for our monster.
- I painted the ribbon-like extensions on the monster's back with some highlight and color.
- I added creases and folds all along the back and head and around the blisters.
- I added highlights to the blisters to make them look wet.
- I painted suckers on the close tentacle with a color similar to the blisters.
- I painted the wet floor or foreground in broad strokes, only generally reflecting the lights and darks of the monster.

**Figure 8.16** The monster has had lots of additional painting done to his face, skin areas, back, tentacle suckers, and just generally everywhere, trying to raise the overall level of detail.

## Softening the Edges

While I was painting the picture, some of the edges were becoming a little too crisp and harsh. I want the overall painting to be softer and not nearly as clearly defined as some of my strokes were becoming. I can use a number of options to soften the overall look and feel of the painting.

- I can use the Soften effect, but I really don't want to blur the image; I just want to soften it a bit.

- I can duplicate the whole image, apply the Soften effect to the top layer, and then lower that layer's Opacity setting to give a softness to the whole piece. The effect looks a bit like a soft-focus photograph. While this is not a bad effect, it is generally used for more romantically inclined imagery. I don't want my monster to be romantic.

I am going to use Adjust Dye Concentration from the Effects > Surface Control menu. This effect is nice to use when you want to add just a little bit of noise to the image. Painter does not have a noise filter like Photoshop, but you can achieve almost the same look using Adjust Dye Concentration.

1. Select a paper texture from the Papers palette. Choose Sandy Pastel Paper as your paper texture, which is a Painter default. The paper texture will drive the effect.

2.  From the Effects menu, select Adjust Dye Concentration. An option box opens with three controls and the preview window. Change the default settings to the following:

    - Using: Paper
    - Maximum: 100%
    - Minimum: Between 80% and 83%

    Notice how the image in the preview window changes (Figure 8.17).

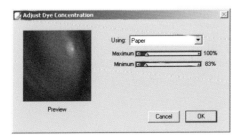

**Figure 8.17** The Adjust Dye Concentration options box

You do not want a very dramatic effect in the preview window. In this case, subtle is much better.

3.  When you're satisfied with the image in the preview window, click OK.

The whole image is softened just a bit by adding some noise based on a paper texture to the painting. The details are not lost as they would be if the image were just blurred (Figure 8.18).

**Figure 8.18** The whole painting with added noise based on the current paper texture. The overall effect is one of softening without blurring the details.

As I continue to paint, some of this texture will be lost. This is not a great concern, because I will just add that texture back in the final step of the painting process.

I continue to paint on the monster and extend his detail off the right side of the painting. I made this change because the character was feeling unbalanced. I finish painting most of the detail into the far tentacle and soften the edges of the monster's face so that the edges merge into the shadows.

## Adjusting the Foreground

I really don't like what's happening with the foreground. We need to give the monster a little elbow room and give ourselves a little more room to work.

1.  Using the Canvas Size command from the Canvas menu, add an additional 200 pixels to the bottom of the image. This gives you more room to work as you paint the foreground, and it makes the monster not feel as crowded by the edges of the painting.

2.  Repaint the entire foreground area, eliminating the beginning reflections. Paint with the three brushes we've been using all along: Dons brush, Opaque Round, and Glow.

3.  Switch to the Grainy Water brush, and blend all the colors. Grainy Water is a great default blending brush that you can find in the Blenders category.

Figure 8.19 shows all the work on the monster as well as the painting and blending on the foreground.

**Figure 8.19** A lot of painting is done on the monster, and the foreground is repainted and blended.

For all intents and purposes, the character is finished, but something more definitely needs to be done about the foreground.

## Painting the Foreground

While the monster is finished, the painting cannot be considered complete until the foreground is finished.

I like the idea of a reflection to give the environment a wet feeling, but I don't like how the initial reflection is working out. I decide to use one of the techniques described in an earlier chapter to create a reflection of the monster in the foreground. This should give the very wet look that I am after.

To create the reflection of the monster in the foreground, we will do the following:

1. Select the whole painting.
2. Copy and paste the painting back into itself, creating a new layer with the whole painting on it.
3. From the Effects menu, choose Orientation > Flip Vertical.
4. From the same menu, choose Free Transform and scale a flipped layer so the layer is only as tall as the foreground (Figure 8.20).
5. With the Reflection layer active, choose Focus/Glass Distortion from the Effects menu.

**Figure 8.20** The whole image is copied, pasted, flipped vertically, and scaled in the vertical dimension in preparation for creating the reflected monster.

**6.** When the options box appears, enter the following settings in each of the controls (Figure 8.21):

- Using: Paper.
- Softness: About 11.
- Map: Refraction.
- Quality: Good.
- Amount: About 1.
- Variance and Direction: Default.
- Click OK.

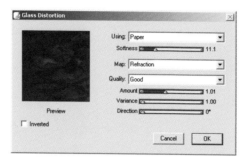

**Figure 8.21** The Glass Distortion option box

A nice reflection of our monster is now added to the foreground, and the painting is basically finished (Figure 8.22).

**Figure 8.22** The reflection of the monster

# Finishing Touches

The painting is 99 percent finished at this point. But I never seem to be satisfied and want to make a couple of final adjustments to the piece.

I want to add a little slime to the monster.

1. Just in case you make a mistake, create a new layer to paint the slime.

2. After you create the new layer, use Dons brush and paint some slime hanging from the back tentacle. Let the background show through, and paint only the dark areas and the highlights. I'm not really concerned about the realism of the slime, and actually it is added more as a subtle point of humor to the rather grim painting (Figure 8.23). After all, who can't laugh at a little slime?

**Figure 8.23** Slime is added hanging from the back tentacle.

One of the last things I want to do is set the monster's head into a darker area shadow to add a bit more mystery. We can accomplish this easily using the Apply Lighting effect.

3. Choose the Apply Lighting effect from the Effects > Surface Control menu. In this case, I use the default Warm Globe preset. Applying this effect results in a painting where the head is in deep shadow while the body maintains its bright color and intensity (Figure 8.24).

4. The last touch is to once again use the Apply Lighting effect, but this time use the Splashy Color preset.

You can see the finished painting in Figure 8.25.

**Figure 8.24** The Warm Globe preset in the Apply Lighting effect is used to push the monster's face into darker shadows.

**Figure 8.25** The finished painting

## Final Thoughts

This painting is probably the least technical of all the paintings in this book. It shows a quick method you can use to take a piece of concept art to the final painting. More than anything, speed is the main consideration when doing this kind of work. Just because you will paint quickly does not mean you cannot paint work that is of high caliber and quality.

I hope that you can use this rather straightforward technique in your own work. Quite often in the digital art forums that you find online, this technique could be called speed painting. While it is not quite as quick as a color sketch, it does take significantly less time than the other tutorials demonstrated in the book, with results that are significantly more refined than just a color sketch.

# Painting Shiny Baubles

*This final chapter is about painting shiny things. There is often a need when digital painting to paint shiny objects. Shiny objects are no harder to paint than other objects; you just adjust the values differently. There are a few tools in Painter that make painting shiny objects easy.*

*This chapter looks at several of the methods I might use when painting shiny jewelry or other highly reflective objects in a painting. In this particular case, I'll be painting imaginary jewelry on a stylized figure.*

*There are, of course, as many different ways to paint these types of objects as there are objects to paint, but the basic underlying principles are the same regardless of the artist.*

# 9

**Chapter Contents**

## Using a Different Approach

This chapter is set up differently from most of the others in the book. In earlier chapters, you saw the progression from the first steps of an image to the last. This tutorial also shows a progression from the beginning of a painted face until the finishing touches, but the order in which the individual elements are painted is not important. Feel free to move between sections as you like.

The techniques that I use to paint this image are applicable to any shiny subject matter.

This chapter also assumes that you know more about Painter than previous chapters assumed. Earlier chapters may have specified an opacity or setting, but in this chapter, much of that is left up your own discretion.

The painting is approximately 2000 pixels square. The color scheme I wanted to use for this painting was based on greens and purples. When the initial image was created, I set the paper color to a nice mid-value olive green. When painting flesh tones, olive green is a nice complement to the skin colors.

With the paper color set as the background color, I erased to the green color instead of to white. This makes corrections much easier in some paintings.

## Painting the Face

Since the object of this tutorial is not about painting a face, I've already finished most of that work.

I painted this face from my imagination and stylized it in a way that would work with the jewelry to be painted. In this case, I did not use a scanned sketch as a basis for the face.

Painting the face was quite straightforward using Dons brush and the Opaque Round brush. I painted the subject on a new layer above the background. With the Picked Up Underlying Color box checked, I was able to let my brushes blend subtly with the background color.

Because we will be using a technique that mirrors some of the jewelry pieces, we want a face that is very symmetrical.

1. Create a new layer.
2. Paint half the face.
3. Copy that half face.
4. Paste the half face back into the image.
5. Flip the new layer horizontally.
6. Carefully align the two halves.
7. Collapse them to one layer.
8. Paint over any seams and imperfections.

There are, of course, certain areas where a simple mirroring will not work or produce the results we want. For example, simply mirroring the eyes would result in highlights on the eyes that would indicate two light sources in different directions.

Obviously, this would be unacceptable and confusing to a viewer, so we need to paint areas like the eyes individually.

You may have also noticed how very long the neck appears. I did that on purpose. You'll learn why in a later section.

I kept the face on a separate layer from the background during most of the painting. Figure 9.1 shows the painting used in this tutorial.

**Figure 9.1**  The face painting used in the tutorial

Ultimately, the light is coming from above and slightly to the right, and the face is almost symmetrical. The light is ideal for what I want to demonstrate in this tutorial.

You can either use my face painting to follow along or paint one of your own.

**Note:** The layered painter file is available for download at www.sybex.com/go/painter, so you can follow along if you want.

## Adding a Decorative Pattern to the Fabric

First I want to add a little bit of pattern and break up the dark fabric of the robe that the subject is wearing. This is simple to do using tools and techniques demonstrated in earlier chapters: paper textures and the Variable Chalk brush. I want the pattern to be similar to the shapes of the jewelry that I will paint in later stages.

I created several paper textures with overlapping circles. I used circles because they reinforce the shapes of the jewelry that I will create, but I want the pattern in the fabric to add a slightly random element into a very symmetrical painting. The overlapping circles in the paper textures are drawn randomly to achieve this.

If you have not already done so, you can load the paper library that I created when doing this tutorial. The library is called `circles.pap` and has half a dozen different paper textures with random circular patterns.

 **Note:** Circles.pap is available for download at www.sybex.com/go/painter.

1. Create a new layer.
2. Use the Variable Chalk brush to paint the circular pattern over the black robe (Figure 9.2).

**Figure 9.2** A circular pattern is painted on a new layer over the black robe.

3. Slightly blur the pattern using Effects > Focus > Soften. Leave the setting at the default when the option box opens.
4. Lower the Opacity setting of the layer to 50% (Figure 9.3).

While I want a pattern to be noticeable, I do not want it to be distracting. Adjusting the amount of opacity is a good way to decide how visible the pattern will appear.

5. Use the Eraser tool to clean up the edges of the pattern.
6. Duplicate the layer and increase the brightness of the duplicate layer.
7. Erase areas of the Bright layer, leaving some light and dark contrast in the pattern.

**8.** Collapse the two Pattern layers together.

**9.** Collapse the Pattern and the Face layers.

A nice random circular pattern has been added on top of the dark robe, and the painting is now ready for the addition of some jewelry (Figure 9.4).

In the next section, we'll start adding some jewelry to our painting.

**Figure 9.4** A subtle pattern has been added on top of the robe.

## Painting the Earrings

In this section, we will begin to add some jewelry to the painting. We will paint several large hoop earrings using Align to Path, a new feature in Painter.

Align to Path constrains your brushstroke to a vector path or shape in Painter. The result is somewhat similar to stroking a selection but much more controllable and variable.

When you stroke a selection, a brushstroke is painted along the edges of the selection without any variation in the stroke. There's no ability to vary the opacity, width, or color of the stroke.

When you use the Align to Path feature, not only can you vary the width, opacity, and color of the stroke, but you can also change the paper texture and even the brush itself.

You can control how closely the brush will follow the shape using a Preferences/Shapes menu. A higher tolerance setting aligns a brushstroke more closely to the shape (Figure 9.5).

The Align to Path button is found in the Property Bar when the brush tool is selected (Figure 9.6).

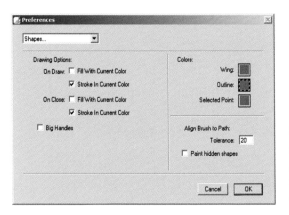

**Figure 9.5** The Shapes menu, where you can specify how closely a brushstroke will align to a path. The higher the setting, the more accurately the brush will align to a path.

**Figure 9.6** The Align to Path button in the Property Bar

Now that you know where the Align to Path button is located, let's add some earrings to the painting.

1. Pick the Oval Shape from the toolbox and draw a long, thin vertical ellipse (Figure 9.7). The ellipse is drawn very thin to look like it is hanging from the ear parallel to the side of the face.

It does not matter if the shape we draw is filled with a color. The Align to Path button constrains a brushstroke to the edges of the shape. We can set both the stroke and the fill for our ellipse in the Property Bar. I chose a bright yellow stroke and no fill so the shape would be very visible against the background.

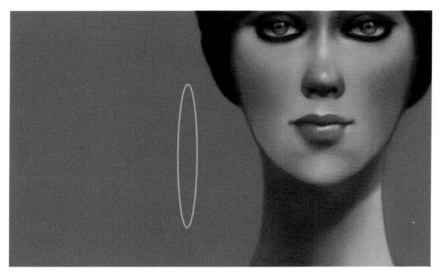

**Figure 9.7** A long thin vertical ellipse is drawn using the Oval tool.

**2.** Click the Align to Path button and, using the Jewelry brush, drop mid-valued gray around the oval.

A new layer is automatically created. The brushstroke conforms to the oval shape on the new layer and we will not be able to paint anywhere else in the image (Figure 9.8).

**Figure 9.8** A new layer is automatically created and the brushstroke is constrained to the oval shape on the new layer.

The Jewelry brush is a simple brush created just for this tutorial. It is available for download at www.sybex.com/go/painter along with the other resources for this chapter.

**Note:** The Jewelry brush is available for download with the other resources for this chapter.

3. Unclick the Align to Path button.

4. With the painted Oval layer active, Load Selection from the Select menu. Leave all the options at the default settings, and click OK.

5. Create a new layer above the painted Oval layer and set the Composite Method to either Gel or Multiply. The selection is still active, as shown by the marching ants.

6. Using a Digital airbrush, paint a darker gray over the top and bottom portion of the selection (Figure 9.9).

**Figure 9.9** Darker gray is painted over the top and bottom areas of the selection on the new layer.

For this next step, we need to decide which side of the earring will be oriented toward the front of the face, with the opposite side toward the rear of the head. In this case, I decided that the outside edge of the earring would be oriented toward the front of the face. It really doesn't matter one way or the other.

7. Pick the Eraser tool and erase the dark gray on the top left and bottom right of the layer that was just painted (Figure 9.10).

**Figure 9.10** The top-left and bottom-right dark grays are erased on the new layer.

8. Collapse the Dark Gray and Gray layers together.

9. Click the Align to Path button.

10. Choose the Glow brush, and paint some highlights down the center of the Earring layer. Use a slightly larger Glow brush on the top edge and bottom edge of the earring to add a strong highlight (Figure 9.11).

11. From the Effects > Focus menu, select Soften and add a slight blur to the earring (Figure 9.12).

**Figure 9.11** The Glow brush is used to add highlights down the center of the Earring layer as well as strong highlights on the top and bottom earring edges.

**Figure 9.12** A subtle blur is added to the earring using the Soften effect.

The earring is finished. We need to position it so it looks like an earring and not a floating loop of metal.

12. Duplicate the Earring layer so we have one for each ear.

13. Flip one of the Earring layers.

**14.** Position each of the earrings under each ear (Figure 9.13).

**Figure 9.13** Each one of the Earring layers is positioned under an ear.

**15.** When the two Earring layers are positioned as you want, collapse the layers into one Earring layer.

This step is optional, but I find it easier to work if I keep the number of layers in any given image to the minimum needed.

**16.** Use the Eraser tool to erase the top of each earring so it disappears into the shadows on the side of the head (Figure 9.14).

**Figure 9.14** The top of each earring is erased so it appears to fade into the shadows on the sides of the face.

That is all there is to painting large hoop earrings. It is made quite easy using the Align to Path feature available with Painter's brushes. Not only is Align to Path useful when painting jewelry or shiny objects, but any time that greater control is needed when painting. I have seen it successfully used with industrial design subject matter all the way through medical illustration.

We will go ahead and add a couple more earrings using the same technique just for practice and to solidify the procedure. This time the earrings will be wider so they do not appear to be hanging in the same plane as the first pair.

1.  Create the new oval using the Oval Shape tool (Figure 9.15).

**Figure 9.15** The beginnings of the second set of earrings using the Oval Shape tool.

2.  Using the same technique described earlier, paint a pair of earrings, and position them next to the first pair. Because they are on separate layers, you can try putting one pair in front of or behind the other (Figure 9.16).

**Figure 9.16** The second set of earrings is finished and positioned on top of the earlier set.

Now that the earrings are finished, I am going to add some silver neck rings in the next section.

## Painting the Neck Rings

We are going to paint a series of neck rings on the figure. This type of adornment can be seen on women in the Paduang tribe of Thailand. It is fascinating to see women wearing this piece of jewelry. It appears to stretch their neck, though in reality it presses their shoulders down. Painting the effect is a challenge.

I mentioned earlier in the chapter that I had painted the neck on the figure way too long. Now you know why.

### Creating the Neck Rings

Painting a series of neck rings on the figure is similar to painting the earrings. In fact, the technique is identical except for the way you set up each ring to be in perspective. You cannot simply draw one ring, duplicate it several times, and expect it to look correct.

We will start from one end and work to the other. Whether you start at the chest and work to the chin or at the chin and work to the chest is not important. We will start at the chest and work up.

It is easiest to use shapes without a color fill when drawing these ellipses. Uncheck the Fill box in the Property Bar when the Oval Shape tool is selected to remove the colored fill.

1. Use the Oval Shape tool and draw an oval shape over the bottom of the neck at about the clavicle level.

2. Pick the Jewelry brush, and click the Align to Path button in the Property Bar.

3. Draw along the front part of the oval path with a mid-value gray color (Figure 9.17).

**Figure 9.17** The oval shape positioned over the lower neck with a gray stroke over the shape.

There is no need to draw the complete ellipse, as we would have to erase the parts behind the neck. No reason to create more work for yourself than necessary.

4. Change the Composite Method of the painted oval to Screen. The gray color lightens and becomes semitranslucent.

5. Duplicate the Oval Shape layer.

6. Scale the duplicate oval shape slightly smaller in width and height using the Layer Adjuster tool.

7. Paint another band using the same gray, and change the Composite Method to Multiply. The new layer becomes quite dark.

8. Select both the Shape layer and the Multiply layer. Move them up using the Layer Adjuster tool so the bottom of the Multiply layer touches the top of the Screen layer.

9. Duplicate the second shape again, and scale it once more slightly smaller in both dimensions.

10. Paint another band of gray, change the Composite Method to Screen, and move both the shape and painted stroke up so their bottom touches the top of the previous Painted layer.

11. Continue duplicating the shape, painting the band, changing its Composite Method and alternating between Screen and Multiply, and arranging both the shape and layer above the previous pair until they cover the bottom of the chin.

12. Hide all the shapes but do not delete them, as they are needed to paint the highlights on each ring.

The arrangement of alternating rings should look something like Figure 9.18 and be quite flat at the chin and rounder at the clavicles. Though the rings appear light and dark, this is only because their Composite Methods are different; they are actually the same color.

**Figure 9.18** The rings around the neck appear as alternating light and dark shapes because of their Composite Method.

1. Change the Composite Method of each of the rings back to the default.

2. Pick each shape in succession, and paint a lighter gray center stripe down the middle of each gray ring.

**3.** Choose each ring, and add a small shadow using the Effects > Objects > Create Drop Shadow menu item. Use the following settings to offset a small shadow below and slightly to the left of the ring (Figure 9.19).

- X-Offset: **–2 Pixels.**

- Y-Offset: **2 Pixels.**

- Opacity: Default **63%.**

- Radius: **3 Pixels.**

- Angle: Default **114.6.**

- Thinness: **45%.**

- Check the box Collapse to One Layer.

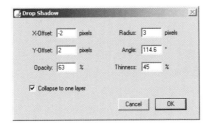

**Figure 9.19** The settings in the Create Drop Shadow option box.

The image should now look similar to Figure 9.20. The rings are starting to look silver but are still quite flat.

**Figure 9.20** he rings around the neck have been changed back to the default Composite Method, and a light highlight has been painted on each using the Align to Path feature.

4. When all the individual rings are positioned correctly, select them and group them. It is not necessary to include the shapes in the grouped layers.

5. Duplicate the ring group.

6. Collapse one of the ring groups into a single layer. The second group is kept as a backup but can be hidden from view.

7. Select the Neck Ring layer, and carefully erase the rings that cover the chin. It is easier to see what you are erasing if you lower the Opacity setting of the layer or change its Composite Method to Multiply or Screen.

8. Duplicate the Ring layer.

9. Change the Composite Method of the top Ring layer to Multiply.

10. Lower the Opacity setting of the Multiply layer to around 50%.

11. Use the Eraser tool and carefully erase everything but areas on the rings that would be in shadow (Figure 9.21).

**Figure 9.21** The chin of the figure is now visible, and a shadow has been added to the neck rings.

12. Use the same technique to add some highlights to the rings. Instead of changing the duplicate layer's Composite Method to Multiply, change it to Screen. The rings are now lighter, and everything but the highlights can be erased.

13. There are now three layers: the basic Ring layer, a Shadow layer, and a Highlight layer. Select all three layers and collapse them to one Ring layer.

## Turning the Neck Rings Silver

While the rings are now starting to look like metal, they look more like pewter than silver. To make them appear silver, we need to add some color to the rings. Shiny objects almost always reflect the colors that are around them, and it is no different in this painting.

If we carefully paint the following colors into the neck rings, the illusion of silver will be greatly enhanced: the maroon color from the robe trim, the flesh colors, and the background color.

Using a combination of Dons brush and the Opaque Round brush, paint color into the following areas on the silver rings:

1. Paint the flesh colors into the bottom half of the rings on the light side of the figure.

2. As the rings turn into the shadows, replace the flesh color with the maroon color found in the trim on the robe.

3. Paint the background color reflecting onto both the right and left side of the rings that are perpendicular to the viewer.

4. Pick the Glow brush, choose a bright orange color, and paint some glowing highlights onto the light side of the neck rings.

The neck rings are now finished. They appear colorful and very shiny. They should look something like the rings in Figure 9.22.

**Figure 9.22** The finished neck rings

In the next section, we will paint shiny jewelry using the Liquid Metal Plug-In layer.

## Using Liquid Metal to Paint Jewelry

The Liquid Metal Plug-In layer initially looks like an interesting toy with limited use. For a long time, I thought the same thing. I avoided using the tool except when giving demonstrations on features in Painter that no one uses.

Since then, I have used the tool extensively in different paintings to paint jewelry and other shiny objects. I have used it to effectively paint rain drops on a window as well as drops of blood. It is a very useful and effective tool when used with a little imagination.

The easiest use of Liquid Metal has to be painting highly reflective jewelry. In this section, we will use it to create some of the glittering beads, the silver necklace, and the metallic hat pin on the turban.

### Accessing the Liquid Metal Plug-In Layer

The Liquid Metal Plug-In layer is at the bottom of the Layers palette. It and a number of other Plug-In layers are accessed by clicking the small icon that looks like an electrical plug (Figure 9.23).

**Figure 9.23** The location of the icon that opens the list of Plug-In layers

Clicking the icon brings up a list of available Plug-In layers. At this time, we are only interested in Liquid Metal. Selecting the Liquid Metal option automatically creates a new Dynamic Layer and opens the Liquid Metal palette (Figure 9.24).

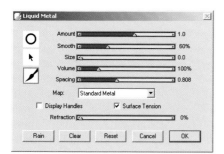

**Figure 9.24** The Liquid Metal palette

The controls available to the artist include the following:

- A circle icon is for drawing individual circular elements.
- The arrow icon is used for moving individual liquid metal elements.
- The brush icon allows the artist to paint with liquid metal.
- A number of different sliders control the amount of reflection in the metal drops.
- Map accesses a drop-down list that determines what is reflected in the drops.

We will be using Clone Source as the map. The clone source defaults to the active pattern unless another image is set as the source.

The remaining controls in the palette will stay at their default settings.

- The Display Handles box is unchecked in the default mode.
- The Surface Tension box is checked in the default mode.
- A Refraction slider is not moved.
- Several buttons are used to accept the effect, clear it to start over, reset the layer, and create a rain effect (Figure 9.25).

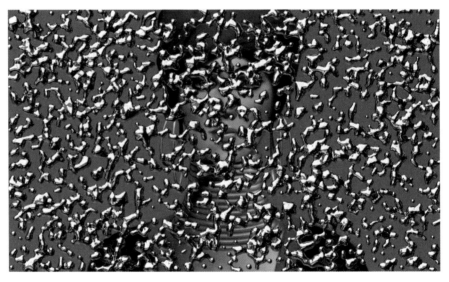

**Figure 9.25** The Rain button has been clicked to apply the Liquid Metal to the Dynamic Layer.

As you can see from the image, a metallic series of drops is applied randomly to the new layer. I recommend that you experiment and play with Liquid Metal.

The key to using the Liquid Metal Plug-In layer is creating custom reflection maps instead of relying on the default ones that come with Painter. Any custom reflection maps can be loaded into the Patterns palette using the Pattern Mover.

I have made a number of custom patterns to use in this tutorial. They are available to download at www.sybex.com/go/painter if you have not already done so.

### Painting Jewelry Using the Liquid Plug-In Layer

We will use the Plug-In layer to create a hat pin for the front of the turban as well as some beads to be used in other areas around the painting.

1. Select Liquid Metal using the Plug-In Layers icon.

2. Using the circle icon in the Liquid Metal palette, draw several drops of liquid metal ranging from large to small. Do not draw them close together, or they will attract each other and distort the circular shape (Figure 9.26).

**Figure 9.26** Several large and small drops of liquid metal are drawn using the circle tool. There are seven chrome circles on a new layer.

3. Duplicate the Dynamic Layer four or five times.

4. Right-click the first Dynamic Layer, and commit it to a default layer.

5. Hide this first layer.

6. Double-click on the next duplicate Liquid Metal layer.

7. Pick one of the new patterns from the Patterns palette.

8. Select Clone Source from the drop-down menu.

9. The Dynamic Layer updates, showing the currently active pattern reflected into the drops (Figure 9.27).

10. Right-click the layer, and commit to the default.

11. Continue doing the same thing to other layers, trying different patterns.

**Figure 9.27**  The active pattern is reflected into the liquid metal.

There will probably be a number of different possibilities that look attractive. Since we will not need all the layers, we keep only the favorite few. There is no right or wrong choice; your taste should guide your selection of which layers to keep.

Keep the original Reflective layer. The shiny appearance of each layer can be increased using the original layer.

**12.** Move the original layer to the top of the stack.

**13.** Change the Composite Method of the original layer to Screen, and lower its Opacity setting to about 20%.

**14.** Reveal and hide each layer in succession to see how the original Screen layer increases the appearance of shine (Figure 9.28).

**Figure 9.28**  The shiny appearance of the metallic circles can be increased using the original Metal layer set to Screen and the Opacity setting lowered to about 20%.

**15.** Choose your favorite or favorites. If you want to keep more than one set of metallic circles you will need to duplicate the original layer that number of times.

**16.** Collapse the Screen layer and Circle layer for each set you want to keep.

Now that at least one set of metallic circles has been created, a hat pin can be positioned on the turban.

**1.** Choose your favorite set of shiny circles.

**2.** Select one of the larger elements in the set, and copy and paste it back into the painting.

**3.** Hide the original set of shiny circles.

**4.** Move the new piece of jewelry, and position it on top of the turban.

**5.** Create a new layer under the hat pin, and paint a shadow on the skin or fabric depending on the positioning of the top layer (Figure 9.29).

**Figure 9.29** The hat pin is positioned on the front of the turban.

That is all there is to using the Liquid Metal Plug-In layer when creating simple circular pieces of jewelry. Of course, you are limited only by your imagination when using this tool. This section should only be the catalyst for more experimentation.

## Creating Another Piece of Jewelry Using Liquid Metal

Before moving to the next section, we will create another piece of jewelry using Liquid Metal. This time we will draw a variety of shapes and combine them into more complicated pieces. The basic technique is identical, so I will not repeat all the steps to apply custom patterns as reflection maps.

**1.** Create a Dynamic Layer using the Liquid Metal Plug-In layer icon at the bottom of the Layers palette.

**2.** Click the brush icon in the Liquid Metal palette, and then draw a number of random shapes on the new layer (Figure 9.30).

**Figure 9.30** A number of random and quickly drawn strokes using the brush on the Liquid Metal Dynamic Layer

Draw the shapes quickly. Quick strokes give a smoother shape than slow, careful approaches.

**3.** Experiment using different patterns as the Map > Clone Source. When you have a look that you like, right-click and commit the layer to the default.

**4.** Duplicate and flip the layer horizontally (Figure 9.31).

**Figure 9.31** The layer is duplicated and flipped horizontally

**5.** Move the layers together, looking for interesting shapes.

**6.** When you find a combination of shapes that you like, copy and paste the individual pieces onto new layers.

**7.** Move the layers together to form the base of a new piece of jewelry (Figure 9.32).

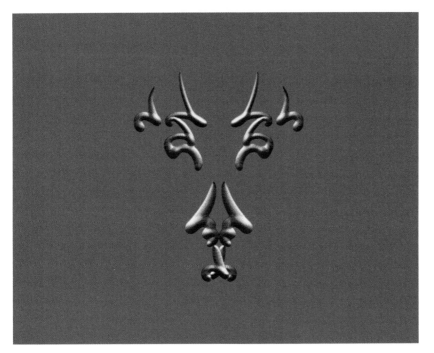

**Figure 9.32** The shapes are arranged as the base form of a piece of jewelry.

8. Use other pieces from the original layers and the circular layers, paint new pieces, do whatever you want. There is no right or wrong approach as long as you, the artist, are satisfied with the result (Figure 9.33).

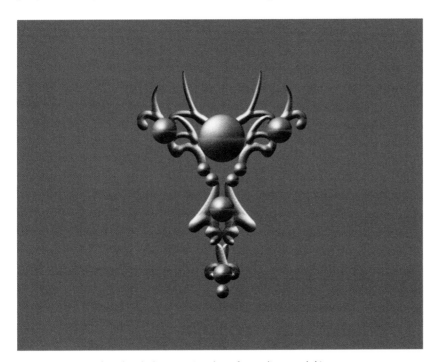

**Figure 9.33** A piece of jewelry is built using various shapes from earlier created objects.

9. When the result is satisfying, collapse the individual layers together.

10. Position the layers over the figure (Figure 9.34).

**Figure 9.34** The new piece of jewelry is positioned over the figure.

We have now used Liquid Metal to create two pieces of shiny jewelry. Remember that the techniques shown are meant only as a starting point for your own experimentation.

In the next section, we will be adding some strange-looking feather-like shapes behind the figure.

## Using a Custom Brush to Paint Decorative Shapes

This section will show you how to create a custom brush and use it to paint Bird of Paradise–type feathers. They are just decorative and not meant to represent anything in particular, but they show the potential of simple brushstrokes with their settings modified.

The original brush used to create these strokes is Dons brush. As you already know, this is a pretty simple brush that makes straightforward strokes used for quick painting tasks. The basic brushstroke looks like Figure 9.35.

**Figure 9.35** Basic strokes
made using Dons brush

## Creating the Custom Brush of Feathers

With just a few quick adjustments to the brush settings, you will have a brush that
produces strokes like those in Figure 9.36.

**1.** Make sure that Dons brush is currently selected.

**2.** Display the Brush controls, which are under the Window menu.

**3.** Change the following four settings:

- In the General settings, set Opacity to 100% and Expression to None.
- In the Size settings, click the second brush profile in the second row of
  profiles.
- Set the Minimum size slider to less than 10%.
- Check the box that is next to the Expression drop-down list.

Currently, pressure is the chosen expression. Checking the box inverts the way
pressure applies the stroke. The default is less pressure/smaller brush size. Checking
the box inverts this so that we have less pressure/larger size.

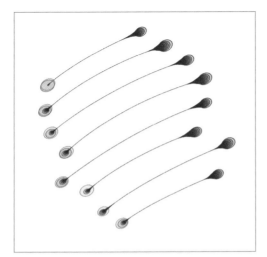

**Figure 9.36** The resulting
brushstrokes after several
simple setting changes

That's it. The brush should now make a stroke that is similar to the one in Figure 9.36.

I really can't think of how to describe the stroke other than that it looks similar to the shape of feathers I have seen in photographs of some species of Birds of Paradise. This custom brush is available in the brush library available for download at www.sybex.com/go/painter.

 **Note:** This custom brush and others can be downloaded at www.sybex.com/go/painter.

4. Use the custom brush to draw a number of quick strokes on a new layer (Figure 9.37).

**Figure 9.37** Shapes drawn using quick strokes just to the side of the face

5. Duplicate and flip the layer horizontally.

6. Position both layers behind the Face layer (Figure 9.38).

7. Copy, paste, and move individual strokes and groups of strokes to get a denser look (Figure 9.39).

8. When you are satisfied with the appearance of the multiple strokes, collapse the entire group of individual feather-like layers together.

**Figure 9.38**   The layer is duplicated and flipped horizontally, and both layers are positioned behind the Face layer.

**Figure 9.39**   Strokes are copied, cut, and moved to achieve a denser appearance.

## Adding Beads

The final touch will be to add some of the smaller shiny circles created with the Liquid Metal to each tip of the feather-like shapes.

**1.** Choose one or several different circles, and place a copy on each tip or each stroke (Figure 9.40).

**Figure 9.40** A small bead has been added to the tip of each feather-like stroke.

We will now use one of the smaller beads to create a pattern that can be used to paint several lines of beads across the turban.

**2.** Use one of the small beads and create a new image that is exactly large enough to encompass the single bead.

**3.** Copy and paste that bead into the new image. It should be on its own layer, with the surrounding areas transparent.

**4.** Load a selection based on that transparency.

**5.** Capture a pattern from the selected layer.

**6.** The Pattern options palette opens. Leave all the settings at their default, and name the new pattern Beads. Click OK.

**7.** The new pattern should be active, with its preview visible.

**8.** Create a new layer above the Face layer.

**9.** Choose the Pattern Pen Masked brush variant from the Pattern Pens category and draw several lines of beads across the turban.

**10.** Load a selection from the newly painted layer.

11. Create a new layer above the beads, and change its Composite Method to Multiply.

12. With the selection still active, paint some mid-value gray on the new layer. It should only paint inside the selection and darken the beads on the layer below.

13. Collapse all the layers except the background together.

The face and jewelry are now finished. A bit of work on the background, and the painting will also be complete (Figure 9.41).

**Figure 9.41**  All the jewelry is finished.

In the next section, we will use one of the more esoteric features to add some interest to the flat background.

## Creating an Amazing Background

In this section, we will use one of the more esoteric features found in Painter to add some interest to the background.

1. Create a new layer below the Face layer and above the background canvas.

2. Fill the layer with white.

3. From the Effects menu, choose Esoterica > Maze.

4. The Maze option box appears (Figure 9.42).

5. Enter 20 into the Thickness box.

6. Click OK. The layer is filled with a complicated maze (Figure 9.43).

Just in case you do not have the time to solve the maze on your own, here is the solution (Figure 9.44).

**Figure 9.42** The Maze options box

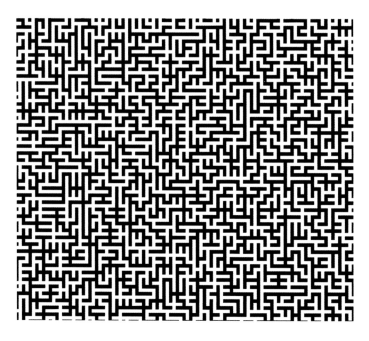

**Figure 9.43** The new layer is filled with a maze.

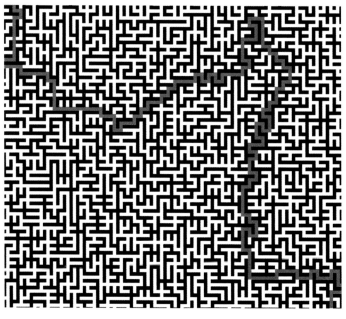

**Figure 9.44** The solution to the maze

You can generate the solution to any maze you create simply by checking the Display Solution box in the Maze Options.

**7.** Create a new layer above the Maze layer.

**8.** Fill the layer with white, and apply a Lighting effect to cover the surface with a rainbow assortment of colors. The custom lighting effect used in this painting is created using the options displayed in the Lighting Options palette (Figure 9.45).

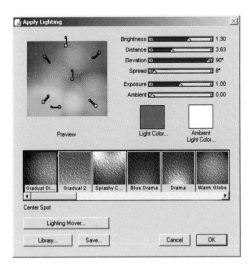

Figure 9.45 The Lighting Options palette showing how the lighting effect was created

You are encouraged to create your own effect, but the custom light library is also available for download at www.sybex.com/go/painter.

**Note:** The Custom Lighting effect preset is available for download www.sybex.com/go/painter.

**9.** A rainbow of color is applied to the White layer.

**10.** Change the Composite Method of the Color layer to Colorize.

**11.** Choose the Maze layer, and select the black lines of the maze with the Magic Wand tool.

**12.** Backspace and clear the black lines from the maze. You can delete the original Maze layer at this time.

**13.** Load a selection from the transparency of the Maze layer.

**14.** Choose the Color layer, and backspace to clear the selected portions of that layer.

**15.** Lower the Opacity setting of the Color layer to 20%.

The image will now look something like Figure 9.46, with the colorized Maze layer above the background.

**Figure 9.46** The image with the colorized Maze layer over the background

**16.** Drop the Maze layer onto the background.

**17.** Apply another Lighting effect to the canvas using the default lighting scheme Warm Globe.

The whole image will now look something like Figure 9.47 with the finished background.

Everything is finished in the painting except one final step.

**Figure 9.47** The background for the image is finished.

## Finishing Touches

Almost everything in the painting is finished at this point. We just need to make one small final adjustment to the face.

1.  Duplicate the face and Jewelry layer.

2.  Apply the Soften effect to the top Face layer.

3.  Reduce the Opacity setting of the top layer to about 20%.

A subtle Soft Focus effect is applied to the image. The painting is finished (Figure 9.48).

**Figure 9.48** The finished painting

## Final Thoughts

This was a rather long chapter, but hopefully it has made painting shiny objects easier and given you plenty of information to inspire you to greater experimentation in your own work.

# Index

**Note to the Reader:** Throughout this index **boldfaced** page numbers indicate primary discussions of a topic. *Italicized* page numbers indicate illustrations.